Antique Roses
for the South

Antique Roses

FOR THE SOUTH

William C. Welch

With Contributions by
Margaret Sharpe and S. J. Derby

Foreword by Neil Sperry

❧

Taylor Publishing
Dallas, Texas

Also by William C. Welch:
Perennial Garden Color

Published by Taylor Publishing Company
          1550 West Mockingbird Lane
          Dallas, Texas 75235

Designed by Whitehead & Whitehead

Photo credits follow index.

Library of Congress
Cataloging-in-Publication Data

Welch, William C. (William Carlisle), 1939–
    Antique roses for the South / William C. Welch.
        p.   cm.
    ISBN 0-87833-723-7 : $29.95
    1. Old roses—Southern States.   2. Rose culture—
Southern States.   3. Flower arrangement—Southern States.   I. Title.
SB411.65.O55W45   1990
635.9′33372—dc20   90-34640
                        CIP

Printed in the United States of America
10   9

To the lovers of the rose, past and present,
and to those Southerners who have
given us this fragrant, gracious, and
beautiful heritage. May we
pass it on in the
same spirit.

For Lilianne
Best Wishes + Happy Gardening!
William C. Welch
4/28/00

Contents

'Céline Forestier'

FOREWORD

BY NOW you've surely seen Bill Welch's first book, *Perennial Garden Color*. It's become one of the most-used gardening references in my library. Judging from its popularity among gardeners, I'm not alone.

Wrapped up between its covers, *Perennial Garden Color* tells the story of the author. It exemplifies the exuberant dedication the man brings to his work every day. Gardening is Bill Welch's hobby. He also makes it his vocation. He is nationally recognized as an outstanding horticultural educator.

As soon as I read his first book, and its section on antique roses, I *knew* there would soon be a second book. I've known Bill Welch for twenty years, and I've admired his love of old roses. I knew that one section of a book wouldn't be enough. I knew he'd want an entire book on one of his all-time favorite flowers.

That's what you have here now . . . the definitive word on one of the most popular groups of plants for Southern gardens. Old roses are riding a wave of immense popularity from home hobbyists, landscape designers, and nurserymen all over America. Bill has included chapters on collecting old roses, planting them into the landscape, arranging them, and using them in crafts. You'll find everything you'll need to succeed with this fascinating group of flowering shrubs and vines.

So, pull up a lawn chair, prepare to make notes, and make plans to plant antique roses into your gardens. You'll start catching that Bill Welch spirit as soon as you turn this page and get on with yet another great work from one of the South's most respected horticulturists. I'm proud to invite you into *Antique Roses For the South*, by my friend, Dr. William C. Welch!

Neil Sperry

ACKNOWLEDGMENTS

An almost instant bond exists among people who love to garden. Sharing plants and information is second nature with the gardeners I know. It is in that spirit of sharing that this book is offered.

This spirit of sharing as well as a dedication to preserving our gardening heritage describe some of the friends who have been instrumental in the preparation of this book.

Pamela Ashworth Puryear of Navasota, Texas, has provided valued research assistance and enthusiasm for my work with old roses and garden history. She also founded "The Old Texas Rose" newsletter, organized the first "Rose Rustle" in our area, and served as editor for the *Heritage Rose Letter* which reaches the national organization of old rose enthusiasts, the Heritage Rose Group.

Margaret Sharpe of Houston is currently editor of "The Old Texas Rose" newsletter and capably provided our section on rose crafts. Margaret devotes a great deal of her time and talent to work with roses and Texas Garden Clubs, Inc.

Well-known for her flower arranging talents, S. J. Derby has focused here on growing and arranging old roses. Her talent and enthusiasm for sharing knowledge about enjoying the beauty and fragrance of these flowers inside our homes has made her demonstrations and illustrated programs a popular choice for civic and gardening groups. S. J.'s photography brightens the pages of her section.

Ruth Knopf of Edgmoor, South Carolina, has provided valuable research and firsthand knowledge as well as beautiful photographs of old roses in the South. Marion L. Brandes of Houston; Cleo Barnwell from Shreveport, Louisiana; Josephine Kennedy, Springfield, Louisiana; Joe Woodard of Dallas; Charles L. Walker, Jr. of Raleigh, North Carolina; D. Greg Grant, Arcadia, Texas; and Stephen Scanniello from the Brooklyn Botanical Garden have all made significant contributions toward making this book a reality.

I deeply appreciate the support and enthusiasm of my colleagues at the Texas Agricultural Extension Service and the Department of Horticultural Sciences at Texas A & M University.

Tom Christopher, author of *In Search of Lost Roses*, has provided valuable editing assistance, as have Mary Hermann Kelly and Arnie Hanson and the entire staff at Taylor Publishing Company.

Last and most I want to thank my wife, Diane, my son, William, and all my family for their patience and support of this work.

The following individuals as well as many others provided valuable assistance with the book and are gratefully acknowledged by the author.

Frances Brandes	Ethel Orr	Deanna and Earl Krause
Bernice M. Smith	Neil Sperry	Brenda Buest Smith
Belle Steadman	Hazel McCoy	Sally McQueen Squire
Mike Shoup, Jr.	Patti McGee	Bob Webster
A. Scott Ogden	Frances Parker	Roberta Churchin
Liz Druitt	Mary Zahl	James David
Vicky Jackson	Amos Welder	Dr. Dorris Brown
Catine Perkins	Robert Richter	Bill Schumann
Miriam Wilkins	Don and Karen Lehto	Nancy Volkman

Holly Shimizu
Suzanne Turner
Scott Purdin
Shingo Woodward
Flora Ann Bynum
Mary Palmer Kelly
Hugh Dargan
Dr. Neil G. Odenwald
Dr. Jerry Parsons
William D. Adams
Tom Le Roy
Dr. J. C. Raulston
Dr. and Mrs. Ed Givhan

R. Elizabeth Williams
Dr. Robert Reich
Dr. H. Brent Pemberton
Dr. Yin Tung Wang
Dr. David Reed
Dean Norton
Peter Hatch
Peggy Newcomb
Harriet Jansma
Keith Hansen
Dr. Robert Basye
Susan Schmidtke
Doug and Rose Mitchell

Vincent J. Mannino
Bob Brackman
Dr. Richard Stadtherr
Nell Denman
Bertie Ferris
Angela and Jerry Fannin
Dr. John Lipe
Mary Knox
Marge Hurt
Joan Stansfield
Renee Blaschke
Joe Woodard

Antique Roses
for the South

Why Old Roses?

BESIDES their charm and beauty, old roses are also tough. In the days before garden hoses, sprinkler systems, and pesticides, these older sorts flourished and, once established, survived on old homesites and cemeteries, sometimes for centuries, without any care. Decades of climatic extremes—droughts, heat waves, hurricanes, blizzards, and floods—and often the bulldozers of real estate developers have killed the weaklings, leaving a select group of survivors: strong shrubs that remain green in the face of adversity. And the majority of these antique shrubs simply sneer at the attacks of insects or diseases.

But old roses have something else to offer the modern gardener—an exceptional, unique beauty. Even when not in bloom, old roses have a naturally attractive form and healthy foliage, and these, together with the fascinating diversity of their flowers, furnish endless opportunities for creative gardening.

What Is an Old Rose?

THE definition of an old rose is somewhat nebulous. The American Rose Society classes as "old" any rose introduced before 1867, but most collectors are more lenient, considering as eligible any rose seventy-five or more years old, if it exhibits typical old rose characteristics. One telltale sign is the unforgettable true rose perfume that lives on in undiluted form in many old roses. Unfortunately, the richness and diversity of these flowers' fragrance is notably lacking in the majority of modern roses.

In addition, old roses are, for the most part, superior as shrubs. Because the modern hybridizer breeds primarily for striking floral colors and an "ideal" blossom form, the shape of the plant itself is generally unremarkable, especially if the gardener is at all casual about pruning. By contrast, old roses have an inherent beauty of form, a quality that does not diminish over the years, and one that makes them particularly useful as landscape plants.

Another characteristic feature of old roses lies in the blossoms' colors. Old rose colors are more muted than those of modern hybrids, tending to pastels. Modern roses, with their

This bloom of "Frances Leake" shows the muted
hues characteristic of antique roses.

brilliant reds and yellows, are more eye-catching than antique roses. Yet after exposure to the older types, many collectors develop a preference for their softer hues. What's more, many old rose varieties also display handsome foliage, while others set attractive hips in the fall which can be harvested for their vitamin C content.

The Historical Perspective

THROUGH the ages, the rose has been considered the queen of flowers. Just where did it originate? Some roses are native to the United States, but the majority come from Europe and the Orient. Rose species native to the temperate zone were long ago cross-pollinated in nature, and later in gardens, to bring about new varieties.

In the late 1700s and early 1800s, European botanists explored the world, searching for new plants of garden value. The roses of their homelands bloomed only once a year, usually in late spring, but in China and other parts of the Far East they found roses that bloomed year-round. The plant explorers named these roses "China" and "Tea" Roses, and brought them back to the West. Enthusiasts crossed the newcomers with their European cousins, the once-blooming Gallicas, Musks, Centifolias, and Damasks. These crosses gave rise to many new classes of garden roses: the Noisettes, Bourbons, Portlands, Hybrid Perpetuals, Polyanthas, and Grandifloras. By the turn of this century, however, the popularity of one class, the Hybrid Teas, with their classic bud form and striking colors, had swept almost every other type off the market.

While those modern hybrids won the praise of the multitude, there always remained a few rosarians who preferred the older varieties. Eighty years ago, the renowned English gardener Gertrude Jekyll extolled the beauty and landscape value inherent in many of the old cultivars. A generation later, another Englishwoman, Vita Sackville-West, featured many of the once-blooming and prized old varieties in her famous garden at Sissinghurst Castle. In the United States, Georgia Torrey Drennan, a Southern woman about whom little is known, wrote a wonderful book about rose culture in the Gulf South. Published in 1912, and no longer in print, it has the cumbersome title: *EVERBLOOMING ROSES For the Out-door Garden of the Amateur, Their Culture, Habits, Description, Care, Nativity, Parentage.* But the text reveals a wealth of firsthand experience and the skill of a knowledgeable horticulturist.

"Martha Gonzales" works well as a landscape shrub.

The movement to preserve old garden roses began in America in the late 1930s with Ethelyn E. Keays. Chatelaine of a Maryland plantation, she began with her sister's help to identify the roses that she found on her own property, afterwards setting out to collect others from her immediate neighborhood. The book she subsequently published provides a distillation of her horticultural archeology, but to taste the excitement of her collecting adventures the reader should turn to the series of reports she wrote for the American Rose Society *Annuals* during the 1920s and 1930s. Another old rose pioneer of this country was Roy Shephard, whose *History of the Rose* (Simpkin, Marshall and Hamilton, Kent & Co., 1903) clarified the distinctions between various rose classes as well as simplifying old rose identification.

As early as the 1930s, nursery operators like Francis Lester of Watsonville, California, had begun to propagate their "found" roses. In 1975, Carl Cato of Lynchburg, Virginia, and

Miriam Wilkins, who lives near San Francisco, helped to found the national Heritage Roses Group, and many interested old rose aficionados found information and inspiration for their own collections. Among the pioneers in the South were Mrs. Cleo Barnwell of Shreveport, Louisiana, Vicki Jackson of New Orleans, Charles Walker of Raleigh, North Carolina, and Ruth Knopf of Edgemoor, South Carolina.

Interest in old roses is increasing today, as Americans seek out these flowers in historic cemeteries, old gardens, and abandoned homesites, where the plants have endured in spite of years of neglect. Rose books written during the nineteenth century are being republished, public gardens established, and organizations formed to provide educational information on this fascinating and diverse group of flowers. Interest has been further stimulated by the naming of the rose as the national flower by Congress in 1986.

The motive for this old rose revival is more than patriotism or nostalgia, however. As old rose collectors know, theirs is a practical passion. In their recovery of the genus *Rosa*'s forgotten treasures, the men and women of this horticultural renaissance are also rediscovering the source of this flower's fame. They are, quite simply, discovering a very exciting, varied, and adaptable group of shrubs, one that deserves far more extensive use in American gardens.

Left. The beauty of antique roses is part of the reason for their growing popularity.

In Search of Old Roses

CHAPTER TWO

A SMALL GROUP of old rose collectors ("rustlers," as they style themselves) gathered in a yard in Anderson, Texas. They stood around a rosebush, admiring its blossoms—luxurious swirls of heavy, pink petals—in awestruck silence as the group's leader, Pam Puryear, went to knock on the door of the modest house. A diminutive, elderly woman answered, and Pam asked, "Could you tell us about your wonderful rose, and could we have some pieces to root?" Mary Minor, the owner of the home, smiled—she knew the rose was beautiful—and told us that a woman in the neighborhood had given her cuttings many years before. All she had ever done by way of caring for it was to scatter some "improvement" (manure) around the bush in wintertime.

Mary Minor's rose proved to be an 1843 Bourbon, 'Souvenir de la Malmaison.' Its flower form is unusual: each cup of spiralling petals divides into

Left. 'Old Blush'

quarters like a heraldic coat of arms. Besides their visual appeal, its blossoms number among the most fragrant in all of rosedom. It's a survivor, too. As Mary Minor testified, this is a bush that will flourish with little or no care through a central Texas summer. If given an open, sunny site and an occasional feeding, this rose will also remain nearly disease-free, which is impressive for a rose of the Bourbon class, a group known for a tendency to black spot. In sum, 'Souvenir de la Malmaison' is an individual, a rose which, once experienced, will never be mistaken for another. Making such discoveries is what rose rustling is all about.

Why Collect Old Roses?

THERE have always been a few people who collected old roses, but this activity has rapidly gained in popularity over the past ten years. One reason that rustlers give to explain their interest in collecting is the impossibility of obtaining from commercial sources many rose varieties introduced in the past 150 years. The availability of some varieties was affected by shifts in taste as to color and flower shape. In addition, quite often varieties that were useful and especially well adapted to specific areas of the nation were dropped by nurseries because they were not generally adaptable or popular for the whole nation.

Cold hardiness is probably the main reason that many of the fine old roses in the Tea and Noisette classes were dropped from widescale nursery production. Disease resistance, longevity, landscape display, shrub form, and flower fragrance were not as important as bud shape and color to rose breeders in the past hundred years. The excitement of discovering varieties no longer commercially available still flourishing in old gardens, cemeteries, or abandoned homesites has made rose collecting a passion for gardeners all over the world.

Another reason for the increasing popularity of old rose collecting is that it can be a very inexpensive pursuit and one to which gardeners can devote as much or as little time as they desire. The names and addresses of several organizations devoted to collecting and growing old roses are listed, along with the sources for plants, at the back of this book. Some of these organizations plan collecting trips and exchanges of plants and cuttings that can be a great help to the inexperienced collector. Although revival of interest in collecting and growing old roses is international in scope, during the past ten years collectors in Texas and California have led the way in organizing groups to offer collectors some support and to further this important and fascinating activity.

Ink Mendelsohn, a writer for the Smithsonian Institution, attended the 1987 "Rose Rustle" at Weimar, Texas. Her husband, Bob, and S. J. Derby, a Houston collector of old garden roses, examine and take cuttings from an old Tea Rose.

The group with which I came upon Mary Minor's 'Souvenir de la Malmaison,' for example, is a Houston-based body organized by Pam Puryear. Originally called the Brazos Symposium on Old Roses, it has come to be known more commonly as the Texas Rose Rustlers because of annual spring and fall forays into the Texas countryside to collect roses. It has grown from a core of about ten people to a mailing list of some two hundred. Groups such as this one include beginners as well as experienced gardeners. Some join because they enjoy the detective and research work relating to the roses they find, while others participate to share information on the culture of old roses.

Membership in these organizations usually costs between five and fifteen dollars annually and includes newsletters detailing members' activities and research relating to the correct naming of collected roses. Collectors never remove plants from the original site, but instead ask for permission to take cuttings. Instructions on rooting cuttings are included in this text (*see chapter six*) and will be helpful for the beginner.

The Making of a Rose Rustler

WHAT follows is the progression of my experiences with collecting old roses. I hope it will encourage you to join one of these groups or start one of your own, and thus help preserve the past and make the future a little richer for generations to come—while adding beauty, fragrance, and living history to your own garden.

My interest in antique roses began innocently enough when, as a child, I enjoyed the small pink blossoms known in my mother's family as the "Fisher Rose." Mr. and Mrs. Fisher lived next door to my Aunt Edna in Rosenberg, maintaining both home and garden immaculately in the German tradition. They were generous in dispensing the interesting plants and vegetables they grew in a landscape that today would be described as a cottage garden. When my aunt admired one of their roses, the Fishers, as a matter of course, gave her cuttings.

Aunt Edna made a hedge of those infant rosebushes, alternating them with bridal wreath (*Spiraea cantoniensis*) down one edge of her property. The spring bouquet the plants provided, the almost azalea-like color mass of the roses combining with the white bridal wreath, was a traffic stopper for many years. But unlike the bridal wreath, the roses didn't quit blooming with the onset of summer. Their display lasted right through the year, except when a hard freeze forced a brief rest; Aunt Edna found that it wasn't unusual for those rosebushes to flower eleven months out of twelve.

I now know those "Fisher Roses" to be specimens of the famous China Rose, 'Old Blush.' This is an ancient variety; portrayal in Chinese art and literature prove it to be more than a thousand years old. When first imported into Europe, in the late 1700s, it caused as much of a stir there with its free-blooming habits as it did in the Rosenberg of my childhood, for it was the first everblooming rose Europeans had seen.

Like most China Roses, however, 'Old Blush' is sensitive to cold, performing best in hot weather. It sulked in the cold, wet climate of northern Europe, and though it served as an important source of breeding stock (it sired many of our modern everblooming garden roses), 'Old Blush' itself did not long remain in Old World gardens. When it arrived in the New World with European immigrants sometime in the early 1800s, however, the rose found in the American South and in Texas a nearly ideal environment. Indeed, it and other China

"Mary Minor," the original plant in Anderson, Texas. This rose was later identified as 'Souvenir de la Malmaison' a Bourbon Rose introduced in 1843.

Above. "Maggie" growing at the gate of Don and Karen Lehto's turn-of-the-century farmhouse near Burton, Texas.

Left. "Maggie" is a rose of unknown origin first propagated by the author in 1980.

Roses are so well adapted to our area that abandoned plants a hundred years old or older can be found growing wild. I know that some of Aunt Edna's original plants, dating from the 1940s, are still flourishing in Rosenberg.

My next encounter with an old rose came at Christmas in 1980, when my wife, Diane, and I visited her grandparents' place in northern Louisiana. Theirs was a real family home: some of the property has been in the family since before the Civil War. I never knew Diane's grandmother, Maggie Traweek—she died the year Diane and I met. But I knew the garden had been a major part of her life. By the time of my visit, shade from overhanging pecan trees and ten years' absence on the part of the gardener had begun to take their toll, but some of the perennials, flowering shrubs, and roses still remained. I admired a red rose that on previous visits had always seemed to have a few blossoms; it was bearing this time, too, even in late December. The flowers were very full and fragrant, and their stems scented the hand of the holder with a distinctly pepper-like odor. I decided to take a few cuttings to see if they would root.

Several of the cuttings did strike root, and they grew vigorously; by early summer they had even borne a few flowers. Late the following fall, I transplanted one, together with a healthy young plant of 'Old Blush' given to me by Aunt Edna, along the front fence of our turn-of-the-century farmhouse in rural Washington County. Both plants thrived in the clay soil and sunny location.

In the years since, our Texas Rose Rustler group has found the rose I collected in Louisiana on numerous sites in Texas, but we have never been able to identify it positively. Until an old rose is identified, tradition rules that it be named for the person from whom it was collected; hence we call this one "Maggie." The name of this rose is in double quotation marks because it is the study name for the rose; single quotation marks are used for names of flowers that have been positively identified.

My experiences with these two hand-me-downs made me realize that not all roses are high-maintenance plants like the Hybrid Teas I had grown previously. I love Hybrid Tea Roses for the beauty of their bloom, but have always felt that their foliage and growth were rather sparse. I've found them susceptible to disease, too. Therefore, I had always kept my roses segregated in a separate bed and had thought them useful only as a source of cut flowers. Now, however, I began to suspect that roses, at least these remarkable foundlings, could play a much broader role in the landscape.

How Old Is Old?

As I dug deeper into this subject, I learned that not all of my finds qualified officially as old roses. The final authority on this matter, at least within the United States, is the American Rose Society, and it defines old roses as those bred before 1867, the year in which 'La France,' the first of the Hybrid Tea class, was released. This does not bother me unduly, since, like most old rose aficionados, I'm not as concerned about dates or definitions as I am about the horticultural value of a plant. If a found rose proves to be hardy and a reliable bloomer, and if the flowers are similar to those of other antiques, then it is welcome to a spot in my garden.

While the history of a rose's lineage is important to collectors, most (like myself) are equally concerned with fragrance, landscape value, and disease resistance. This last, a natural resistance to bacterial and fungal infections, is one of the greatest virtues of the old roses, but it does not automatically come with age. Many of the roses sold a century ago were as prone to disease as any modern hybrid. But it has been my experience that roses found flourishing on neglected or abandoned sites *do* prove trouble-free—any that could not survive without sprays have long since died.

About this time, I was given a catalog from a nursery in California that for many years had been one of the few commercial suppliers of old roses. I ordered eagerly from that beautiful catalog, but found that their roses are budded onto understocks and not grown from cuttings, and so lacked the durability of my homegrown heirloom roses. Budded roses are actually two varieties growing together, a hybrid top (or scion) grafted onto the roots of an understock, a rose of some other tough but unspectacular variety. If a hard winter should kill a budded rose back to the ground, the shoots that emerge from the roots the following spring will be those of the understock; the hybrid flowers for which the gardener bought the bush are gone forever. An own-root rose, by contrast, a rose grown from a cutting like my collected bushes, is all of a piece and so returns with the same flowers it has always borne. Some of the Californian plants did well anyway, though. As our Washington County garden filled with old roses, I began to realize the exceptional landscape potential of these plants: they blended easily, I found, with perennials in mixed borders.

It was then, too, that I joined the Heritage Roses Group, a national organization devoted to the study of old roses. The *Heritage Roses Letter,* this organization's quarterly newsletter, proved to be a good source of information and of contacts with other old rose collectors. With the resurgence of interest in these old-time flowers, more and more sources of information are becoming available. For instance, in Texas, *The Old Texas Rose* newsletter gives gardeners in the central part of the state the latest information about old roses. And Dallas area enthusiasts and many others enjoy *The Yellow Rose,* a monthly newsletter on antique roses. Following their lead, the book publishing industry has begun in recent years to reissue nineteenth-century handbooks and catalogs. Many of these are beautifully illustrated as well as informative, and the originals qualify as valuable antiques in their own right.

The Joys of Collecting Your Own

MOST old rose admirers sooner or later turn from buying their stock to collecting it themselves. As they do so, their gardens fill with memories as well as plants: memories of new and old friends, lovely fragrances, long-departed loved ones, and the circumstances surrounding all these things. To me, a colorful, well-planned garden is sterile and meaningless unless it also contains these memories. I cannot see cupped, creamy 'Fortuniana' blooms, for example, without remembering a most successful rustle in which we found a specimen of it climbing the porch of the oldest home in Brazoria County, the Ammon Underwood house in East Columbia, a structure that dates to 1835.

Time has added even more associations to this rose. In a recent letter Laura Underwood Cooper, a descendant of the man who built the house, informed me that the 'Fortuniana' we found was probably planted before the Civil War. "At that time," she explained, "the house faced the river, and . . . was much larger. Soon after the war . . . it was discovered that a fissure ran beneath the house. Ammon called in contractors who said the house was too large to move. He then sent for the Negroes who worked on his plantations and they succeeded in their task.

"In the moving, the house was altered so what had once been its back was now facing the river. Although it was moved back more than the width of the river, it has twice more been necessary to move it to save it from the ravages of the Brazos. . . . Family history says that the 'Fortuniana' was moved with the house all three times and replanted in the same

Rosa fortuniana in the garden of Mrs. Mattie
Rosprim in College Station, Texas

position in relation to the gallery. Reportedly, it was a mature rose the first time it was moved, hence my belief that it was planted before the war. It survived each time, although it was certainly not moved at optimum times.

"When my dad was a boy, my great uncle, John Underwood, quite the eccentric, learned how to graft and went on a binge, grafting everything in sight. He worked his magic on a portion of the old 'Fortuniana,' and for years it bloomed both white and pink at the same time. It was reportedly quite a sight, and people came from miles around to see the spectacle."

I was particularly fascinated by Ms. Cooper's information about the use of 'Fortuniana' as an understock for grafting. A friend of mind, Dr. Robert Basye, prefers this rose above all others for that purpose. Dr. Basye has been breeding roses for more than fifty years, and some fifteen years ago he retired from teaching mathematics to devote all his time to the work of returning disease resistance, good shrub form, and fragrance to roses. He contends that, generally, modern roses have been inbred for too long, and to achieve his goals he reaches back to species (wild or native forms) and early hybrids.

Dr. Basye speaks of 'Fortuniana' with great reverence. He uses young, cutting-grown plants as understocks for all his new seedlings and vows that, for our part of the country, there is no better understock in the world. Evidently other growers in Florida and Australia agree, because 'Fortuniana' is frequently cited as a good understock for those areas as well. Dr. Basye will be interested to know that other Texans before him have experimented with grafting this fascinating rose, which was originally brought from China to England in 1845 by the famous Scottish plant explorer Robert Fortune.

Exploring Out-of-the-Way Places

M<small>Y</small> hunt for old roses has taken me to many corners of my native landscape that I probably would not otherwise have explored. Cemeteries, for instance, I have found to be outstanding repositories of old roses, as well as the ultimate proving ground for the bushes' durability. Once planted by a gravesite, a rose, in times past, might flourish undisturbed for generations, its growth checked only by its susceptibility to weather, insects, or disease. Unfortunately, though, this is changing. With families so busy and scattered today, responsibility for maintaining plots is passing from family members to cemetery staffs, and the grounds-keepers have little stake in preserving the landscaping. Many roses and perennials have been mown, grubbed out, or killed by chemical weed controls in the last twenty or thirty years. Fortunately, a few cemeteries have escaped this sign of our times and serve as preserves for the favorite plants of generations past.

A fine example of this is the Evergreen Cemetery in Victoria, Texas, which was the focus of a 1989 rose rustle. Organized by Marion Brandes of Huffman, this event attracted more than fifty participants who carefully searched the extensive grounds of this old grave-yard. Victoria is close to the port of Indianola which, though now largely flooded and abandoned, was the point of entry for many of the German and other new settlers to Texas during the 1840s and 1850s. Though the rustle came in the throes of a major drought, the rustlers nevertheless discovered many fine specimens. This was not surprising in light of Victoria's special dedication to this flower: known as a "city of roses" for many years, the community has recently reinforced that image by establishing a fine municipal rose garden which includes many of the old varieties.

In travels outside my home state, I've found Louisiana to be fertile territory for old roses. Drought is less of a threat there. Indeed, the abundance of the rainfall is more likely to be the problem. By encouraging rapid, lush growth of vines and brush, the moisture helps these competitors overrun roses on abandoned or neglected sites and starve the bushes of sunlight. Perhaps for this reason, my best finds in Louisiana have been in gardens.

For example, near the village of Springfield, some sixty miles east of Baton Rouge, I came upon the fine collection of old roses that Josephine Kennedy has been assembling for many years. Through her generosity I was able to add to my garden several roses that have since become favorites. 'Mrs. B. R. Cant' (1901) is one of these, a wonderful Tea Rose that is also one of Mrs. Kennedy's favorites. The specimen beside her front porch has become a large shrub seven or eight feet tall and nearly as wide.

Another collecting experience in Louisiana took me to Natchitoches. Pronounced Nak-uh-tish, this is the oldest city in the Louisiana Purchase and certainly one of the most beautiful. Alluvial soils from the Cane River, and the city's favored location in the west central part of the state, provide excellent growing conditions. Not surprisingly, the cemetery there, which includes graves dating to the late 1600s, has been a favorite haunt of rose collectors for many years. I came away with cuttings of a wonderful everblooming rose I named "Natchitoches Noisette." The small flowers are cupped as they open and pink in color, with the outside petals often stained much darker. Its fragrance is excellent, and it always becomes a

A red China Rose of unknown origin at the
Evergreen Cemetery, Victoria, Texas

favorite of those who grow it. Yet in the six years I've been growing the rose, no one has been able to trace its true identity.

On the same foray, I stumbled across a small garden on the east side of town that was literally filled with roses. Mrs. McClinton promptly answered the knock on her door and cheerfully allowed me to take cuttings of a highly perfumed pink Tea which was blooming well, though it was then the Christmas season. She had rooted the plants, she told me, from cuttings given to her by a friend many years before; she too, had given away dozens of plants, rooted cuttings, and bouquets. "McClinton Tea" remains one of my favorites today, though it has also defied identification.

Searching for the San Antonio Rose

ONE rose hunt I remember as particularly exciting was the search for the rose to be named the "San Antonio Rose." This 1987 rose hunt was instigated by Greg Grant, the County Extension Horticulturist for Bexar County. After moving to San Antonio, he had become fascinated by the wealth of antique roses in the older parts of that city. He decided to conduct a contest to identify the oldest rose in the city, and at the same time to select an old variety to be named the official San Antonio Rose. With the full cooperation of the media and a commercial sponsor, Greg succeeded in attracting some very unusual entries.

An elderly gentleman submitted a specimen of 'Lamarque' (a Noisette Rose of 1830), that, through various recollections, he was able to document as being ninety-seven years old. This bush, the oldest to be uncovered, was not in good shape at the time of the judging—it had been badly abused in recent years—but it soon demonstrated the resilience of the old varieties. For as a result of the publicity, it received some minimal care and responded enthusiastically, once again blooming beautifully. When Greg and his fellow judges went to inspect this rose, they found an unexpected dividend on the site, too—a large bush of 'Louise Odier,' a Bourbon Rose of 1851.

Neither of these roses, however, took the title of San Antonio Rose. After spending most of two days inspecting the various entries, the judges unanimously agreed that the honor should go to 'Mrs. Dudley Cross,' a Tea Rose of 1907. They chose it for the same characteristics that have endeared it to several generations of San Antonio gardeners. 'Mrs. Dudley

Right. Mrs. Josephine Kennedy in her Springfield, Louisiana, garden with her original plant of 'Mrs. B. R. Cant.'

Top. "Natchitoches Noisette" was found in the old cemetery with graves dating back to the 1600s in historic Natchitoches, Louisiana.

Above. "McClinton Tea," a Tea Rose from Mrs. McClinton's garden in Natchitoches, Louisiana

Cross' is thornless, it blooms nearly all year, it roots easily from cuttings, and it is very disease resistant. The pale yellow and blush pink coloration make it a visual asset in any garden setting.

As interesting as the winners, at least for an old rose collector, was one of the also-rans, a Gallica that was given the study name "Canary Island Rose." Gallicas are frequently found in old cemeteries of the South; they are, as a rule, very long-lived, though their susceptibility to powdery mildew and their habit of blooming just once a year (in the springtime) have limited their appeal to the rosarians of modern Texas. Nevertheless, they are gorgeous roses with a wonderful fragrance. This particular specimen had arrived in San Antonio many years before with immigrants from the Canary Islands. The immigrant rose had rooted well, forming a large thicket of canes. This in itself suggests that the bush started not as a purchase

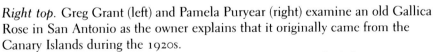

Right top. Greg Grant (left) and Pamela Puryear (right) examine an old Gallica Rose in San Antonio as the owner explains that it originally came from the Canary Islands during the 1920s.

Above. The same rose ("Canary Island Gallica") photographed the next spring

Right. "Canary Island Gallica." Gallica Roses bloom only during the spring but are heat and drought tolerant and sometimes are found on abandoned homesites and cemeteries.

Left. 'Mrs. Dudley Cross' growing in a neglected San Antonio garden was judged the "San Antonio Rose" during a summer 1988 contest coordinated by County Extension Horticulturist Greg Grant.

from a nursery but as a rooted shoot or "sucker" taken from a treasured rose left behind in some Old World garden. Gallicas spread in this fashion only when grown on their own roots; when propagated by budding and grafted onto an understock, Gallicas confine themselves to compact shrubs.

Collectors and Preservers

I n the decade that I've been pursuing old roses, many new recruits have joined the quest as word has spread about the landscape value, historical interest, beauty, and fragrance of these plants. Commercial sources of old roses have sprung up in response to these flowers' renewed popularity, making it possible to buy literally hundreds of varieties. I am grateful for these sources, but I still contend that the best roses, those that will perform best in your garden, are roses that have been on trial for a hundred or more years of drought, floods, insects, disease, heat, and cold in your area, and have survived the test.

Still, it is easy for collectors with sophisticated cameras, specialized libraries, and support organizations to forget that the collector would be of little importance were it not for the preservers of the rose. Most preservers will probably never write scholarly articles, or even care to read one. Yet it is the preservers' love of beauty and the years of attention they have given their bushes that have left us something worth collecting. Moreover, it is their generosity and willingness to share that make these treasures available at all. Their preserved roses are a gift that goes on giving into the future. What greater praise can be given than to say that one has been a good steward, transmitting the beauty of the past to a future which will perhaps sorely need such qualities?

Right. This Texas woman is ninety-four years old and tends her roses and other plants on a daily basis.

Landscaping with Old Garden Roses

CHAPTER THREE

HOW OFTEN we associate roses with visions of sparse, standard bushes standing at attention in vast beds of cultivated soil—or worse, in vast beds of weeds. But that need not be. Handled with a bit of imagination, roses, at least the older varieties, can fill any number of niches in the garden. Actually, antique roses are very versatile garden plants—after all, diversity is in their blood. Garden roses developed from crosses of many widely differing wild species, and though this diversity has been, for the most part, bred out of modern roses, it survives in the older types. A look backward, at how these shrubs were used in the gardens of the past, should convince gardeners of the rose's usefulness. More important, it should suggest many "new" applications for today's gardens.

For the convenience of home landscapers, the following pages have been organized not around historical themes, but around the various uses of old

Left. This parterre at Tudor Place in the Georgetown area of Washington, D.C., effectively features 'Grüss an Aachen' roses combined with perennials.

roses. In each section, the names of a few appropriate varieties have been included. If those selections don't satisfy you, simply turn to the lists of "Suggested Roses for Various Landscape Needs" appended to chapter seven.

Landscaping Using Supporting Structures

Trellises and Espaliers

TRELLISES can be attractive structures themselves, and with the addition of climbing or rambling roses, their effect can be spectacular. Like old roses, trellises are especially suitable for use around many older homes, since they were common features of both classical revival and Victorian architecture. Again like roses, trellises changed style with the period; the builders of classical revival homes favored plain, square designs, while Victorian carpenters preferred more fanciful patterns that echoed details of the "gingerbread" used as trim elsewhere on houses. An entirely different kind of trelliswork appeared between 1910 and 1930, when trellising was separated from the house and used to form arches over garden seats; these arches too were commonly planted with roses or other climbing plants.

An interesting and easily constructed trellis of treated lumber and wire displays 'Variegata di Bologna' and other old climbing roses at the Herb Garden in the National Arboretum in Washington, D.C.

Top. A forty-plus-year-old specimen of
'Climbing Cécile Brünner' has become
so large that it requires extra support in
this San Antonio garden.
Above. Climbing high into a pecan
tree, 'Mermaid' creates considerable
interest at the former home of
Mitzi van Sant in Austin, Texas.
Right. Trellises and pillars covered
with roses in the Cranford Rose
Garden, Brooklyn Botanical Garden.
'May Queen' is the pillar rose.

Left. 'Old Blush' climbs a trellis at Nimitz State Park in Fredericksburg, Texas.
Above. 'Meg' espaliered on a wall at Sissinghurst in England
Right. 'Anemone Rose,' sometimes known as "Pink Cherokee," is espaliered on an east-facing wall at the author's home.

In the past, trellising (or treillage, as it is technically called) offered an instant, inexpensive alternative to the costly garden walls that were favored as a backdrop for backyard plantings. Today, however, trellises more often appear in side yards, where they serve as screens to provide privacy and shade. Because of the continuing popularity of this type of garden feature, ready-made trellises of metal or wood are widely available, but these often appear badly out of scale in the landscape. Fortunately, it is possible to combine economy with a more pleasing effect, since do-it-yourself trellises tailored to your situation are easily constructed from treated pine, redwood, cedar, or similar durable woods. The simplest technique is to make a frame out of two-by-two- or two-by-four-inch lumber and then face it with prefabricated panels of trellising. For an even more custom-designed look, you can construct the panels yourself, so that you can space the lattice to fit the scale and needs of your individual landscape situation.

If trellising is beyond your budget, but you like the architectural effect it provides, you can achieve something similar through an ancient technique known as espaliering. Developed for use with fruit trees, espaliering works equally well with climbing roses. Planted at the base of a wall or fence, the roses are tied in at intervals to the supporting structure. Their canes are then forced, through binding and regular pruning, into a sort of living trellis. Creating a finished espalier will require a couple of years, however, and this treatment is not ideally suited to healthy growth. Roses require both full sunlight and good air circulation, and if the wall should interfere with either of these, it will favor infection by mildew, black spot, and spider mites. Selecting varieties with a natural resistance to these problems increases one's chances for success.

A classic use for climbing roses is to train them as a frame around windows and door-ways; this is not only the simplest treatment of these plants but also one of the most attractive. Another appealing variation is seen in England, where roses are sometimes trained up a wall and onto a piece of treillage on the roof. Though well worth duplicating, such effects are not easy to achieve in our region, since only the hardiest roses will tolerate the sunlight and heat reflected from a wall or roof during a Southern summer. The best choice for this use would be one of the species climbers, or an exceptionally hardy hybrid such as 'Cècile Brünner,' 'Lamarque,' 'Lady Banks' Rose,' 'Mermaid,' 'Fortuniana,' or 'Zéphirine Drouhin.'

Arches and Pillars

BECAUSE rose-covered arches are among the most dramatic of garden features, you should take a certain amount of care in siting one—they make such a strong statement that everyone will notice if they speak out of turn. An arch is a threshold, and you should set it where it invites the viewer into or out of the garden. It should be over a path and at a garden entrance or exit. It is important, too, that an arch be made of materials compatible with other garden features, and it is critical that it be in scale with its surroundings. This is the reason that the ready-made arches sold by mail often disappoint their purchasers: once as-

Right. Noisettes are excellent for use on arches over garden entrances. Here, 'Lamarque' graces the entrance into the cottage garden at the Antique Rose Emporium. Hinkley's yellow columbine is in the foreground. *Left*. Red rambler roses covering metal arches give a feeling of enclosure to a section of the Cranford Rose Garden.

Antique roses, perennials, and herbs are beautifully combined in the Herb
Garden at the National Arboretum in Washington, D.C.

sembled, the arch proves too small to fit the setting. Any arch must provide height and width
sufficient to accommodate the drape of the rose or vines trained over it. In general, allow a
minimum height of about eight feet to the structure's highest point and width of five to six feet.

In selecting a rose with which to clothe your arch, keep in mind that foliage is as important as flowers. Stiff-caned, woody climbers may look fine on a fence or wall, but they do not
adapt gracefully to the curve of an arch. Instead, consider the more flexible Noisettes, climbing Teas, and various ramblers.

Another architectural element ideal for displaying climbers is the pillar. This feature
can serve two purposes: a row of pillars can enframe a garden, but they also make excellent
showcases for choice specimens. Generally, the pillars themselves are made of wood and are
rustic in style. No fancy craftsmanship is necessary; the trunk of a cedar or some other small
conifer makes an excellent pillar, especially if stubs of branches are left as supports for
the roses.

When training a rose onto a pillar, wrap the canes around it in an ascending spiral. This
treatment encourages flowers to "break" from every node of the canes and brings a far more
generous bloom than will result if the canes are trained straight upward. Be sure when wind-
ing the canes to make the first wrap close to the pillar's base, so that the whole length of it
will be covered with roses. This method insures a solid cylinder of blooms—not just a few
sprouting at the top.

Above. 'Louise Odier' is sometimes used as a pillar rose. The support for the rose is the trunk of a small cedar tree. Some of the branches were shortened and left attached to provide support for the rose.
Right. 'May Queen' is trained as a pillar at the Cranford Rose Garden.

Wrapping the canes around in a
spiral encourages full bloom.

'Prosperity' forms a tepee of roses.

Gertrude Jekyll, the famous English horticulturist who revolutionized garden design in the early twentieth century, used to connect rose pillars with swags of chain or very heavy rope. This gave her pillars an added dimension—she could arrange them in arcs, circles, or rows to provide an elegant and unusual method for visually enclosing space within the garden. Vigorous ramblers are best suited to this use.

Another alternative to the basic pillar is to group rustic posts by threes, lashing or nailing them together at the top to make a tepee of roses. Or you can make a rose umbrella by training a climber such as 'Cecile Brünner' up a central column and out over an umbrella-shaped support. The Walsh Rambler 'Excelsa' is often found trained this way, especially in Irish cottage gardens.

Pergolas

A GARDEN pergola is in effect a covered alley. Such structures are a traditional feature of large formal gardens, but they can be adapted for use in today's residential landscapes as well, where they furnish an excellent way to exhibit climbing roses. In a small garden, shorten the pergola to two or three posts, making it a deepened archway rather than a long, covered walk. As a rule, pergolas are most effective if set on level ground and allowed to follow a straight line. They can, however, also be used to emphasize an intersection of two paths—just set a cross-shaped pergola over the spot where the visitor pauses to choose which path to follow and which of your gardens to visit.

A pergola of concrete pillars and wooden laths provides support for climbing roses at the Huntington Botanical Garden in California.

An arched pergola at La Roseraie de l'Hay les Roses
near Paris makes a dramatic feature.
Right. 'White Lady Banks' roses trail down and
soften a tall retaining wall along the River Walk
in San Antonio.

Depending on the effect at which you are aiming, you can fashion pergolas from a variety of materials. Iron and wood are two popular choices. Depending on the pergola's style, wooden timbers may be finished or left rustic. Brick pillars supporting wooden or iron arbors are a long-lasting, if expensive, alternative, and I've seen pergolas constructed with concrete formed to resemble rustic timbers. The paths beneath may be surfaced with brick or gravel or left as grass. To cover the finished structure, you can plant almost any rambler or climbing rose. If you decide to plant a once-flowering variety, you may want to alternate these bushes with everblooming types, to give your pergola a more extended display. For the most spectacular show, however, cover the entire structure with a single variety of rose.

Ground Uses of Antique Roses

Banks and Groundcovers

On a sunny bank, loose, sprawling shrub roses or trailing varieties can furnish beautiful groundcovers. They can make a fairly care-free cover, too, once the roses have thoroughly blanketed the area. The difficulty is in keeping such plantings weed-free while they are establishing themselves. Spreading a thick layer of mulch around the young shrubs helps, although the gardener will also want to keep a thick pair of gloves on hand. Roses suitable for this purpose include many of the Wichuraianas (such as 'Silver Moon' and 'Petite Pink Scotch') and other ramblers, and certain of the species roses such as the Banksias (both 'Alba' and 'Lutea'), and 'Swamp Rose.' *R. fortuniana* can be very effective when allowed to tumble over a wall, especially when a pool of water lies below.

Mixed Borders

A TRADITIONAL and effective use of old garden roses is to plant them in wide borders, mixing them with small flowering trees, shrubs, perennials, and annuals. In designing an arrangement of this sort, try to group the roses together in a block of three or more of the same variety, since that gives them more visual impact and allows you to avoid the spotty effect that can result from series of single specimens. To reduce the risk of foliar diseases such as black spot, be sure to allow enough space around each rosebush for it to enjoy free air circulation. Shrubby, upright sorts like Teas, Bourbons, Polyanthas, Chinas, Hybrid Perpetuals, Hybrid Musks, Noisettes, and many of the species roses all lend themselves to use in mixed borders. By carefully combining these shrubs with other ornamental plants, you can achieve striking combinations that produce color most of the year.

Hedges

ALTHOUGH they can be quite beautiful, rose hedges are best used sparingly because they require relatively intensive maintenance. They look best if shaped periodically with a pair of clippers or shears, although they should not be clipped as closely as boxwood or privet. Here, too, a sunny location with good air circulation is essential to success.

For a relatively low hedge, three or four feet high, use one of the Polyantha or China Roses, such as 'Marie Pavié,' 'La Marne,' 'The Fairy,' 'Old Blush,' or any of the various red Chinas. Hybrid Musks serve for a five- to seven-foot hedge; good prospects include 'Ballerina,' 'Penelope,' 'Cornelia,' 'Felicia,' and 'Belinda.' For a really large hedge, select one of the species roses. Personal favorites are the white and yellow forms of the 'Lady Banks' Rose,' which make huge mounding plants up to twenty feet in diameter and twelve to fifteen feet tall, yet requires little maintenance.

A mixed border at Lehto Farm in Burton, Texas

Old roses, perennials, and fruit trees combine to make the Pleasure Garden
at Mount Vernon interesting and colorful.

If security is your goal, try one of the thorny ramblers such as 'Mermaid' or 'Cherokee,' or one of the Multiflora Hybrids (such as 'Seven Sisters,' 'Vielchenblau,' and 'Carnea'). These will knit their branches together into an impenetrable barrier that also affords a habitat for various bird and animal species. Such a planting may be unusual today, yet it is hardly new. In the 1860 edition of his *Southern Rural Almanac*, Thomas Affleck, the famous nurseryman of Natchez, Mississippi, and Gay Hill, Texas, extolled the virtues of a 'Cherokee' rose hedge for the way in which the branches interlace to form a fence or wall strong enough to keep animals in or out.

Remember when planning your hedge that, if sufficient space is available, staggered, double-row plantings are more appealing than straight rows of bushes. How far apart you should space individual roses within a large hedge varies with the type of rose you've chosen; dwarves such as 'The Fairy' should be set about two feet apart, while the Banksias, 'Mermaid,' and others you'd use for a large hedge should be set at intervals as great as ten or twelve feet.

You'll simplify maintenance and insure a harmonious picture if you use only one kind

Left. A hedge of 'Cécile Brünner' provides a unifying element at the Huntington Botanical Garden.

Above. A hedge of the China Rose 'Archduke Charles' creates a background for a mixed border of seasonal perennials at the Antique Rose Emporium. Landscape design by Nancy Volkman and the author.

Right. 'Cherokee Rose' was recommended as a hedge plant for Southern farms by Thomas Affleck in the 1850s.

Rosa palustris scandens, better known as the 'Swamp Rose,' is used as a specimen at the entrance to the author's home.

of rose for the whole hedge. You can achieve interesting effects, however, by combining several types. If you do, you'll find that planting in blocks, setting three or more bushes of each kind together, gives the most satisfactory effect.

Specimens

ALTHOUGH it's customary in modern gardens to segregate roses together in a bed all their own, old roses, because of their more interesting forms and foliages, also work well as specimen plantings. An occasional large rose, for instance, can be very effective as a specimen in a shrub border, and you may wish to plant a number as specimens within an area of lawn.

Large specimens are also useful for screening unsightly views and for covering dead trees or stumps. Roses with a distinctive weeping form, such as the 'Swamp Rose' or 'Ballerina' (a Hybrid Musk), are particularly attractive as single specimens, as are other types of Hybrid Musk Roses.

'Marie Pavié' is an excellent choice for container use since it is
thornless, reblooms constantly, and is highly fragrant.

Container Gardening with Old Roses

THIS is an historic technique that is peculiarly appropriate to our crowded age. Ground space—a bit of earth in which to plant—is in short supply in urban (and even many suburban) environments today. For gardeners in those areas, containers, which may be set on a terrace, balcony, or even rooftop, furnish a very practical substitute. But container growing offers advantages to any rose grower. When carefully selected and placed, container roses can add either formal or informal appeal to a garden. In addition, container growing allows the gardener complete control of soil, watering, and placement of plants. Indeed, because most containers are relatively portable, growing roses in this fashion enables the imaginative gardener to move and recombine bushes periodically and so take advantage of seasonal displays.

Container-grown plants do have a significant disadvantage in that they usually require more maintenance than those planted directly in the ground. Because the container artificially restricts their root zones, container roses require more frequent watering and fertilizing, especially if you wish to keep your plants in top condition. Roses in containers are also more susceptible to damage from extremes of cold or heat since the roots are elevated above ground and are more exposed to the elements.

Both aesthetic and practical factors will dictate the choice of containers. Unglazed clay pots, for example, may suit your taste better, but they generally require more watering than do glazed ones, because water and air move right through the relatively porous clay. Whiskey barrel halves are the right size for most roses and are often available at low cost. Whatever type of container you choose, however, you must make sure to drill drainage holes through the bottom or sides, since waterlogged soil is fatal to roses. If, for some reason, you must use containers without drain holes, double pot the roses by lining the undrained container with a smaller pot that is equipped with drain holes.

Since the growing medium available to the roots of container roses is limited, it is important that it be of high quality. Packaged potting mixes, which can be purchased in bulk or in small quantities, are a practical choice for most situations. If you prefer to use soil, mix it with liberal amounts of sphagnum peat, compost, or rotted pine bark.

In general, the smaller roses are more practical choices for container growing, although for roof gardens and other special situations, climbers and larger shrubs may be appropriate. Polyanthas such as 'Marie Pavié' and 'La Marne' are personal favorites because they bloom almost continuously through the growing season and may be easily kept within a two- to four-foot size range. 'Old Blush,' the well-known China Rose, is especially effective when combined with prostrate rosemary in a whiskey barrel half or similar size container. Other perennial plants of cascading growth habit such as *Asparagus sprengeri*, lantana, verbena, and dianthus also add a graceful note to a container of roses, as they spill over the pot rim.

'Marie Pavié' is an excellent container plant.

Arranging Old Roses

CHAPTER FOUR

S. J. Derby

No OTHER flower, surely, has contributed more grace and beauty to our gardens than the rose, and in beds and borders this flower has brought centuries of delight to mankind. But old roses have played a starring role indoors as well as out, for as cut flowers their fragrance, color, and beauty have also brought great joy inside the home. From oriental screens to the paintings of Dutch masters, roses are featured, with the floral designer's arrangements enhancing the flowers' native forms and colors. Perhaps this association with treasures of earlier periods accounts for some of the fascination with antique roses that people feel today. Yet these versatile flowers adapt equally well to the simplest of modern settings. With a bit of research and a little insight, anyone can use an arrangement of roses to reflect and enhance the period of any home and its furnishings.

Arranging old roses can be as basic or as complicated as you choose. They

Left. A traditional mass of antique roses makes an elegant statement in an oriental vase.

are very forgiving flowers that may be quickly placed in a crock or pitcher as an informal bouquet, but they function just as well in sophisticated designs in silver or cut glass containers. In the cold climates of northern Europe and the northern United States, such arrangements are a strictly seasonal pleasure, but thanks to the many everblooming roses that thrive in the South, we may have fresh garden roses ten months out of the year.

Basics of Antique Rose Arranging

Conditioning to Make Old Roses Last

ALTHOUGH the diversity of old roses is one of their chief charms, for the flower arranger it presents quite a challenge, since no two varieties behave quite alike. Unlike a modern florist's blossoms, many old roses are short-lived in arrangements. Some last only a few hours, though others demonstrate greater stamina, remaining handsome for several days. An added complication for the arranger accustomed to the roses now used by florists is the fact that many of the old varieties differ from modern Hybrid Tea Roses in the texture of their blossoms, producing thin petals of little substance. Finally, even blossoms that belong to the same old rose class may vary in their responses to refrigeration and conditioning. As a result, it is only through trial and error that the arranger can determine which old roses should be cut in advance and conditioned, and which perform better if cut just when needed and arranged immediately.

The standard technique for conditioning roses (preparing them for use in an arrangement) is to cut the blossoms in early morning, when the buds are nearly closed, that is, no more than one-third open. At this time, remove all foliage except for one or two leaves. After bringing the roses into the house, recut the stems while holding the cut ends underwater. Cutting in this manner prevents air bubbles from entering the stem and blocking its circulatory system, a condition that will cause the flower to wilt prematurely. If recut properly, roses maintain freshness because water will completely fill the stems, leaves, and blossoms.

After recutting the stems, let the roses stand in deep, tepid water for several hours in a cool place before arranging them. Always keep the flowers in a cool, draft-free area until you are ready to use them, since high temperatures and direct sun quickly take a toll. Take care, too, that the water into which you set the roses, both during conditioning and as you arrange

Right. 'Champneys' Pink Cluster' in an antique cut glass basket—perfection floating in space

Below. The arranger's materials (counter-clockwise from the left): plastic liner with oasis and floral tape, butterfly flower cutters, floral clay, clippers, wire, candle pick, corsage tape, cup holder and pin holder, and orchid tube.

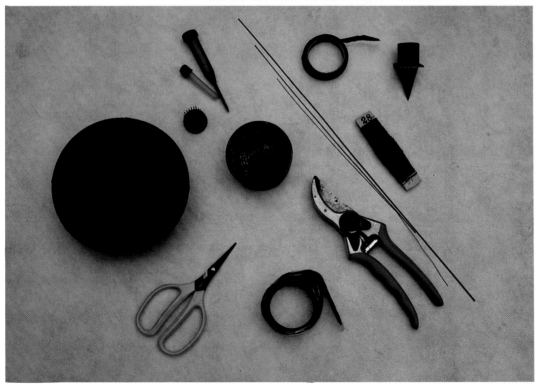

them, is fresh and pure. Use only rainwater or distilled water for this purpose, since most tap water contains sodium and other substances that will shorten the blossoms' life.

Another easy way to prolong the life of your antique rose arrangement is to add a floral preservative to the water. Research has shown that these preparations can double the useful life of cut flowers. You'll find commercial brands of preservatives at retail florist shops and the floral concessions in supermarkets, or, if you prefer, you can make your own by mixing an equal quantity of 7-Up drink (not diet) and water. If you do decide to concoct your own preservative, be sure to let the mixture stand long enough for most of the air bubbles to dissipate before adding it to the completed arrangement. Otherwise, bubbles may slip into the stems and all your care in recutting may be wasted.

To decorate your house for a party, you may need more roses than your garden can supply all at once. You may be forced to spread your cutting over several days to accumulate a sufficient quantity of blooms. In such cases, the refrigerator can serve as a useful conditioning tool. Again, cut the flowers early in the morning. Stand them in a small quantity of water or wrap them in plastic and set them on the refrigerator's lower shelf. Be sure also to remove all fruit such as apples or pears from the refrigerator, since, as they age, they release ethylene gas, a natural ripening agent that will cause roses to drop their petals. Take the flowers from the refrigerator as you need them and proceed as above, starting by recutting the stems underwater.

As mentioned, old roses are temperamental flowers that may not respond well to conditioning. If a variety will submit to this treatment, however, you'll find that it lasts far longer in your arrangement. 'Paul Neyron,' for example, the Hybrid Perpetual of 1859, conditions beautifully: its six-inch, rose-pink blossoms hold well afterwards and last several days when arranged. The luscious 'Mme. Isaac Pereire,' by contrast, drops every petal upon refrigeration and resists all efforts at conditioning. It lasts better, although still not well, if picked just when needed. Somewhere in between is *R. chinensis* 'Mutabilis,' a rose that is magnificent in arrangements. Half of the time it conditions well, and the other half it collapses, for no apparent reason. Other outstanding roses that tolerate conditioning are 'Souvenir de la Malmaison,' 'Sombreuil,' 'Cécile Brünner,' a number of other Polyanthas, and most Hybrid Musks, notably 'Skyrocket' and 'Prosperity.'

As you prepare your roses for arrangement, keep in mind that the other materials you may wish to use—flowers and greens—also need conditioning. Stand these extras in deep water, or submerge their foliage entirely. Exceptions are broadleafed evergreens and tropical materials, which last exceptionally well in or out of water.

Dry branches frame a
magnificent bloom of
'Louise Odier.'

Plants for Line, Filler, and Form

AN unstudied handful of roses may look impressive enough as you carry it in from the garden, but for a more sophisticated arrangement—one with a stronger, clearer form— you'll need two other elements as well: line and filler.

Line elements serve as the bones of an arrangement, establishing form and rhythm. You'll find a wide range of materials useful for this purpose. Bare branches make some of the best line materials when working with old roses. Either green or dry branches will serve, but the younger, more pliable ones do have this advantage: if tied into position while still green, they'll keep to the line you've chosen after they dry. Wisteria, clematis, and ivy are a few of the vines which add line to an arrangement. Blade-like foliage including iris, liriope, or gladiolus leaves can perform the same function. Cattails, dock, grasses, and grains found by the roadside can give strong emphasis to the linear interest of an arrangement, while spike flowers or foliage may also enhance its form. For variety, you should try perennials such as physostegia, lythrum, or perennial salvias, since these harmonize well with old roses.

Filler elements, as the term suggests, are the small flowers or foliage that you use to flesh out the basic outline you have created with line material and roses. Fillers are used primarily in traditional, rustic, or period arrangements, and may consist of many types of materials. Branches of broadleafed evergreens work well for this purpose, as do sprigs of herbs (rosemary is excellent), ivies, and ferns. As you fit filler in among the roses, though, remember that it must remain subordinate to the dominant focus of the floral design.

When choosing filler, also keep in mind that if the arrangement is to be modern, other forms are needed. Tropical flowers and foliage (or even those such as pittosporum that are not, botanically speaking, tropical but share a similar look) have a bold, dramatic form suitable for modern arrangements. Some common materials with this impact are croton, canna, fatsia, caladium, and aspidistra.

Containers

COLLECTING old roses, you'll find, leads naturally to collecting vases, pitchers, and bowls—indeed, all sorts of containers, old and new. Once you've made a habit of showing off your old roses in arrangements, you'll want just the right container to exhibit each variety to best advantage. Compatibility is the key. You may have eyes only for your roses, but,

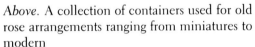

Above. A collection of containers used for old rose arrangements ranging from miniatures to modern
Right. 'Basye's Purple Rose,' 'Belinda,' and roadside materials are grouped to create a modern mass arrangement.

inevitably, the object holding them becomes part of the floral statement, too. So make sure the container you select reinforces the message your arrangement is sending to the onlooker's eye.

Though that may sound complicated, it really isn't. Settle on the style or mood you are aiming at in your arrangement and let that be your guide. For example, the bucolic and romantic connotations of old roses suggest rustic, casual containers such as wooden boxes, kettles, weathered wood, antique copper pots, country china, pitchers, mustard jars, or baskets of all types. The combined effect is charming.

With their historical associations and aristocratic pedigree, however, old roses also lend themselves to period arrangements, and these demand more elegant containers. Cornucopias, classic Greek urns, finger vases, lidded boxes, compotes, English floral china, flower bricks, cut glass, antique silver pieces, and inkwells furnish the right air of antique formality.

If you are truly fortunate, you may have inherited such a container, but barring that, you'll find restoration catalogs to be good sources. Other relatively affordable alternatives are the antique reproductions sold at many museum gift shops.

Many of our old roses originated in Asia, and you may wish to give an Eastern flavor to your own arrangements. Containers for oriental styles of flower arranging include most bronzes, from baskets to usabatas (a traditional Japanese bronze container). You'll find ceramic containers of oriental inspiration at nurseries, or you can purchase them from Ikebana International, a worldwide organization devoted to oriental flower arranging. (For information on how to contact them, see the *Sources* guide in the Appendix.)

Bases

A WELL chosen base increases the importance of the design by setting it off on a platform. The base must be compatible with both the container and the design. Sliced rounds of wood, either treated or left natural, make simple but effective bases, as do wooden rectangles, marble slabs, tiles, fabric, or bamboo rafts. All of these materials, with the exception of fabric, share the characteristics of flatness and natural color. A cloth base has its own advantage in that it allows you to opt for a pattern of colors that picks up a hue in the floral design. It makes sense to try your arrangement both ways, first without a base and then with one. If the intention is a casual look, you may find that a base is unnecessary; it may be a very effective aid, however, in creating a more formal or period look.

Left. Masses of old roses combined with yew and callicarpa berries make a formal statement in a period Greek urn.
Right. A selection of bases used to make an arrangement appear more important

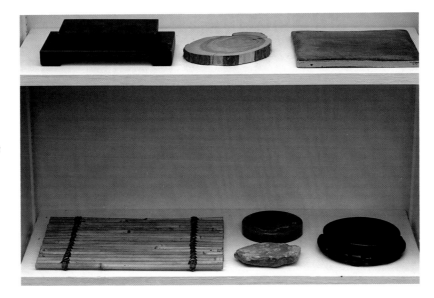

Arranger's Checklist

- Make sure the container, flowers, base, and physical setting for the arrangement are harmonious.
- Put all your materials on the table before starting. Are the sizes compatible? If so, the arrangement will be in good scale.
- Start with the establishment of line to insure that the arrangement has rhythm and provides major interest.
- Place some material facing the back and at the back for depth.
- Place some material below the lip of the container to relate the arrangement to the container.
- For balance, place dark and large flowers low and to the center; place light and small flowers to the outside and top.
- Use variety. Most arrangements need spike and ray (round) forms to be interesting.
- Use a plastic lazy susan or a similar device to turn the arrangement as you work. This insures depth and good color distribution while preventing overcrowding.
- Check your work. Place your arrangement in front of a mirror and look at its reflection to check the form, color, line, and balance.

The following types of arrangements provide a sampling of the many possibilities antique roses provide. Exploring them will add a new dimension to your enjoyment of these flowers. Whether your garden will furnish a hundred cut blooms, or only a couple, there is always enough to bring antique rose fragrance and beauty into your house.

Small Arrangements

Bud Vases

EVEN if your collection of old roses is limited to a single bush, you can still be an old rose arranger. One perfect rose, perfectly displayed, is the simplest yet most dramatic of arrangements. All you'll need for this is a bud vase.

Top. Hybrid Musk 'Bishop Darlington'
in a reproduction Colonial glass whiskey
flask
Above. A grapevine tendril enhances this
miniature arrangement of a bud and
blossom of 'Kathleen,' a Hybrid Musk.
Right. A traditional s-curve line
arrangement featuring the Hybrid
Bracteata 'Mermaid' in a bronze basket

When picking the flower for this display, keep in mind that a bud vase is a feature showcase, so select a quality specimen. Then, before setting shears to rose, calculate the length of stem you'll need and allow a little more—this margin of error will allow you to recut if you want to try arranging the rose in different ways. When you do place the rose in the bud vase, arrange it so that an adequate length of stem and at least one perfect leaf show. Proportion is the important principle, for the beauty of this arrangement lies in the pose of the flower.

For a slightly more complex bud-vase arrangement, choose a bud and one open flower of the same variety. Place the bud high to one side, and the open flower low to the other side, allowing part to hang over the lip of the vase. For the true rose connoisseur, this stunning arrangement offers the virtue of exhibiting a prized rose in two stages of bloom simultaneously. To create more rhythm, add a piece of line material, letting this emerge from the back.

Silver and crystal are the classic materials for bud vases, though they may be made of a variety of other things as well. Bud vases come in a range of shapes but share a basic form: they are tall relative to their width and have a small mouth that admits only a few stems. Bud-vase arrangements are most suitable for kitchen windowsills, cocktail tables, desks, and boudoir vanities.

Miniatures

MINIATURE arrangements, as might be expected, are those made in small containers. Here the main principle to keep in mind is scale, for materials must all be small. Tiny sprigs of monkey grass or grapevine tendrils, for example, are the right size for miniatures.

Your container, too, must be in scale; luckily, miniature containers are found everywhere. An empty shotgun shell provides a rustic detail, while a small bottle or seashell is suitable for more formal use. After selecting a container, fill it with a tiny bit of wet oasis, and use only the smallest buds and flowers. Appropriate subjects include 'Champneys' Pink Cluster,' 'Cécile Brünner,' 'The Fairy,' and 'Nastarana.' Extra care must be expended in keeping the completed miniature arrangement in good condition, because the small size of the container will make it necessary to replenish the water more frequently.

Proper placement is also crucial to the effect of a miniature arrangement. Imagine how lost a five-inch miniature would look in the middle of the dining table: the frame of reference is too large. Focus attention on the arrangement by making it part of a grouping on a table with a figurine, for example, or by placing it in a shadow box at eye level.

Versatility in Small Designs

SMALL arrangements require especially restrained treatment. Because of their size, they need smaller materials and fewer can be included if the design is to achieve a unified effect. Obviously, the container must be small, in keeping with the scale of the arrangement. If the container's neck is narrow, simply place the stems where you want them and the stems will wedge each other in place. With wider-necked containers, use oasis or a flower holder to keep the stems in the chosen positions.

The chief benefit of these arrangements' modest size is their versatility. They grace a windowsill, desk, or small table equally well, and they are just the right size, usually under ten inches tall, to set on a tray or by every place setting as an individual welcome for each guest at a dinner party. In addition, small arrangements are ideal to take to sick friends or send to a teacher at school. If you intend them for these sorts of presents, make your arrangements in small, inexpensive glass bottles, so that the recipient has no obligation to return the container.

Country Casuals

Weathered Wood

WEATHERED wood arrangements are real crowd pleasers and are easy to make—they almost arrange themselves. Their secret is that both the wood and the roses are intrinsically so interesting that the combination is rarely boring.

To construct one of these arrangements, start with any piece of wood that pleases you. It can rest horizontally or sit vertically. Try mounting the wood on a dowel with a base like a piece of sculpture. Attach a block of wet oasis to the weathered wood with sticky floral tape and then insert the stems of roses and other materials into the oasis. Take care to disguise the oasis with either greenery or flowers, since you won't want your mechanics to show. Leave enough of the wood showing, however, for the arrangement to benefit from its rough texture and gray color contrasting with the smoothness, roundness, and color of the roses.

Weathered-wood arrangements offer the perfect chance to carry out your dinner or

Top. Old roses, basil, and oregano arranged in a piece of weathered wood provide the centerpiece for an Italian outdoor buffet.
Above. 'Champneys' Pink Cluster' arranged in a shell.
Left. A country coffeepot makes a charming container.

Two Noisettes, 'Rêve d'Or' and 'Céline Forestier,' combine with late summer perennials and berries for a casual occasion.

party theme. For a Texas theme, try using barbed wire as line material. If you're serving chili, add red chili peppers and white onions by fixing them on bamboo skewers and inserting the skewers into the oasis. Then finish the arrangement with sprigs of some of the herbs that you are using in your recipes.

Rustic Style

RUSTIC arrangements are those that look as if the flowers have been casually placed in a container—a crock or a pitcher perhaps—that the arranger happened to pass on the way to greet guests. But this look is deceptive. Although rustic arrangements are easy, they are by no means careless.

Because they are frequently found blooming in country settings, old roses work perfectly in rustic arrangements. In addition, many old rose varieties are naturally informal in habit, blending easily with wildflowers, weeds, grasses, and other flowers common to rural areas.

If your rustic container is cylindrical, an easy arranging technique is to gather all the materials—roses, grasses, and leaves—in your hand, taking care to include a variety of colors and forms. Begin with the things you wish to rest at the top, and finish with visually heavier materials or those that may hang below the lip of the container. Then, holding all the stems tightly, cut them evenly at the bottom to the height desired. Finally, set the whole handful into the container and let go, letting the stems relax. The virtue of this technique is that it achieves a natural spacing, one that displays the materials to good advantage, while retaining a casual look.

Even if you plan to include only roses in your arrangement, follow the same procedure. Make sure some buds are in the center, and, when you release them into the container, they will all face in different directions. Handled in this way, your arrangement will have a pleasing naturalness rather than a static, soldiers-on-parade look.

For rustic containers with handles, such as baskets or kettles, a good rule is to echo the line of the handle in the lines of the arrangement. Make sure that your line material parallels the handle. If it doesn't, it may set up a broken rhythm, forcing the eye one way with the line of the handle and then another with the line material.

Nowhere in arranging is a riot of colors more acceptable than in the rustic arrangements. Besides, clashes of colors usually are not a problem with old roses because the various flowers are all compatible with one another. The addition of orange gaillardias and yellow rudbeckias, however, may cause one to wince. If you find bright oranges jarring with the pink of the roses, try limiting your palette to old rose varieties that range only from white to pale orange, such as 'Rêve d'Or,' 'Safrano,' or 'Lady Hillingdon.' Also, keep in mind that brighter pinks or rose reds sometimes combine more successfully with yellows than with the blush tints of a 'Mme. Alfred Carrière.' Try to avoid the use of yellow-green foliage, choosing instead plain green or gray-green materials.

Fruit and Vegetable Compositions

Even if you don't own a single container, all is not lost. Anything from apples and pears to eggplants and pumpkins makes an acceptable container for an old rose arrangement. Just core out a section of the fruit large enough to hide a cup holder, insert the cup holder (or

A base unifies this arrangement where fruits and vegetables serve as containers for old roses 'Kathleen' and 'Puerto Rico.'

Simplicity is the theme
of this oriental-style
arrangement featuring
'Rêve d'Or' in a black
basket.

a tin can, in the case of a pumpkin), and add roses. The cup is essential: it not only ensures that your container is watertight, but, by keeping the water clear, it prevents acceleration of the rotting process and a premature collapse of the flowers.

Beyond serving as substitutes for more permanent containers, these home-made ones offer advantages all their own. The colors and textures of natural fruits and vegetables harmonize beautifully with antique roses, and the resulting arrangements are fun. You can achieve a sophisticated look by arranging flowers in a shiny eggplant. For a more casual centerpiece, tuck roses and herbs into a head of lettuce. Or encase the rose stems in waterpicks and slip the blooms into a standing sheaf of asparagus. Turn your imagination loose when working with fruit or vegetable containers—a playful spirit is just the thing to bring these whimsical confections to life.

Traditional Arrangements

Oriental Designing

Rose arrangements in the oriental style should mimic the forms of an oriental painting; achieving balance through asymmetry, they usually emphasize line and space. As a rule, it is a long, beautiful line that initiates the rhythm. Since very few materials are needed to create this linear silhouette, this is an ideal type of arrangement for a season when only one or two roses are blooming. Oriental arrangements are also clean in design and allow for the contemplation of a few carefully selected flowers.

In this type of arrangement, space is of greatest importance and simplicity is essential. Give each rose ample room for its beauty to be appreciated, and keep foliage to a minimum by clipping or pruning so that individual leaves may be seen. At the same time, consider using materials often overlooked in traditional arrangements, such as flowering and fruiting branches. Branches of flowering pear, pomegranates, and callicarpa berries (without leaves) work superbly in the oriental style.

Roses well suited to arrangement in the oriental manner are singles such as 'Mutabilis' and 'Vanity,' which have handsome buds borne on strong, long stems (at least during some seasons of the year), and roses with fine French quartering, 'Sombreuil,' perhaps, or 'Souvenir de la Malmaison.'

Period Pieces

Although period arrangements spring from a genuine interest in historic reconstruction, in most cases they are based on a misconception. Commonly, the arranger in search of authenticity turns for inspiration to sixteenth- and seventeenth-century floral paintings, yet these are works of art rather than historical documents. Most often, the paintings are derived from the artist's imagination rather than actual combinations of cut flowers. Indeed, until recently, little documentary evidence had been uncovered concerning the flower arranging styles of previous eras.

But although such period pieces may lack authenticity, they are rich in charm. Indulge your taste for nostalgia with colonial finger vases, Greek urns, or compotes clasped in the arms of Victorian cupids, and be satisfied to give your arrangements the approximate look of a given period by using only plant materials known to be available at that time.

Your period arrangement should be massed, symmetrically balanced, and geometric in shape. Its outline may be a triangle, trapezoid, or circle. Establish the basic structure first with spiky materials. Then add roses to the design: dark ones to the bottom and center, light ones and buds to the top and sides. Place filler material until the whole arrangement is a solid mass of colors. You achieve interest by varying colors and sizes of roses and by the contrast you create through alternating spiky materials and round rose forms.

Cupid holds a compote full of old roses and rosemary for remembrance. The roses are 'Louis Phillipe,' 'Crimson Glory,' 'Archduke Charles,' "Maggie," 'Ballerina,' 'Cramoisi Supérieur,' 'Maryljlke Cassant,' and 'Clotilde Soupert.'

A Colonial finger vase holds antique roses and nicotiana in an explosion of color.

In style, your period arrangements may be either formal or informal. In a formal period style, you may make effective use of fruit, spilling bunches of grapes over the rim of an urn, for example. An informal arrangement of the colonial period, by contrast, could include grasses and roadside flowers.

Antique roses are obvious subjects for period arrangements, yet curiously, some types present a more convincing picture than others. Among the most effective are cascading roses with nodding heads and a loose, open form, such as 'Mrs. B. R. Cant,' 'Old Blush,' 'Duchesse de Brabant,' 'Mme. Isaac Pereire,' and 'Marie van Houtte'; nowhere else do these old favorites look better. Cluster roses add the necessary variety, and among these you might consider 'Belinda,' 'Ballerina,' 'Lady Banks' Rose,' and the various ramblers. Roses such as 'Jeanne d'Arc,' 'Ballerina,' 'Nastarana,' and 'Russell's Cottage Rose' that bear interesting hips or fruit are appropriate in arrangements of this type.

Pot-et-fleur

Pot-et-fleur (pot and flower) is an exotic French name for what is really a very simple concept. You arrange a few potted plants and some cut flowers in a container and then cover the gaps with sheet moss or Spanish moss so that they all appear to be growing together. As long as the container is properly lined, you can water the individually potted plants as required and replace the cut flowers as they fade. The great advantage to *pot-et-fleur* is that, once you have assembled it, it will last for months with only minor alteration. A *pot-et-fleur* makes a dramatic entry hall statement and a charming hearth or floor accent.

To make an antique rose *pot-et-fleur*, select a suitable container—large brass planters and baskets are excellent—and line it with metallic pot wrap or a plastic plate. Place small foliage plants such as nepthitis, philodendron, or palm in the back of the container. For the front, select ivy, fern, or some plant that will trail over the lip of the container. Tip the pots forward and shim under them so that the plants face you rather than the ceiling. Then set wet oasis or cup holders in between the pots and fill these receptacles with clumps of roses. If the container you've chosen to house your *pot-et-fleur* is a basket, binding its handles with roses will give the arrangement an especially lovely effect.

Potted nepthitis and bird's nest fern provide the framework of a pot-et-fleur that is embellished by a handle wound with 'Prosperity.'

Tea Rose 'Mrs. Dudley Cross' in an antique silver pot with ficus foliage

Silver and Cut Glass

Bотн of these materials seem to have a natural affinity for roses, each enhancing the flowers in a slightly different way. Silver containers, because of their shine, normally dominate any flowers arranged in them. Yet silver complements the velvety texture of roses, especially if the blossoms are set amid shiny foliage materials. Such containers are safe choices for inexperienced arrangers since roses always look elegant in silver, even if poorly arranged. But when choosing a silver container for your arrangement, look for one with a narrow neck and avoid, if you can, a bowl, the hardest shape of all in which to arrange flowers.

The elegant glitter of cut glass complements roses much as silver does, but adds a Victorian touch. A little experimentation will reveal that this remains true whether the cut glass container is an antique or of more recent manufacture. Both cut glass and silver, incidentally, make particularly handsome containers for dining room arrangements since they match the other silver or glass appointments.

Antique Roses in the Modern Home

Multiples

MULTIPLES are modern and dynamic. A practical demonstration that the whole can become more than the sum of individual parts, multiples consist of several arrangements (three or more) grouped together on a table.

In putting together a multiple, strive to make each arrangement slightly different from the others but related in feeling. The success of this synergistic arrangement depends largely on careful selection of compatible containers. Aim to choose containers that are all alike, or all different from each other; matching a few of the containers but not all gives an uncomfortable feeling of indecision. Bottles or ceramic containers that are identical except for size or identical except for color are good choices. Creativity in the placement of the containers is also essential since this contributes to the excitement engendered by the whole composition. Multiples are effective on large buffet or dining room tables.

Modern Forms

MODERN arranging embraces an assortment of subdivisions, all of which share a focus on the creative use of plant material. A walk through a museum of modern art gives one an idea of the range. Many modern arrangements share the characteristics of sculpture, while others incorporate elements of abstract painting. In every case, though, the primary consideration is the placement of bold colors and forms to achieve dramatic effect.

The value of this school of arranging to an old rose collector is the contemporary look it can give to antique flowers. For despite their historic associations, antique roses will fit com-

A massed arrangement of old roses, larkspur, and daisies in a cut glass bowl

fortably into a modern home when grouped as blocks of color with other materials, synthetic or natural, in modern containers. Such arrangements are particularly well suited to entryways or expanses of wall—places where they can express their power and vitality.

The containers used for these up-to-date arrangements are often ceramic and may feature multiple openings so that one can create several centers of interest. Frequently, an arranger will paint or otherwise alter the container to achieve a desired look.

When creating a modern arrangement, select your roses for powerful effect. Bright red cluster roses such as 'Skyrocket' or a dead white rose with the rugged, crinkled foliage of 'Blanc Double de Coubert' make a suitably bold statement.

The Modern Mass

A MODERN mass differs from traditional massed arrangement in its clumping effect. In the modern version, you group roses of the same variety—indeed, each distinct type of material—in a single block. Thus, each type of material retains its identity. The art lies not in blending varieties but in placing the groups in pleasing relationship to each other; traditional placement favors equal distribution of colors and materials throughout the arrangement. This difference lends modern mass arrangements a more powerful impact on the eye than traditional examples have.

Special Creations

Wreaths

WHETHER you intend to hang your wreath on the door or use it as a table ring, it will benefit by the addition of roses. For both dried and green wreaths, the treatment is the same: slip the rose stems into flower picks (these must be replaced daily) and then wire the roses into the wreath, paying strict attention to grouping.

A dried branch and a bold group of 'Grootendorst Supreme' create a small modern arrangement.

'Champneys' Pink Cluster' stars in a bold design in a low raku container.

Boxwood Trees

Boxwood trees are a long-lasting favorite. To make one, cut a large block of wet oasis into a pyramidal shape, shaving off its tip to leave a one-inch square, flat space at the peak. Fit the block to a base, either a plate or a low, round bowl. Soak boxwood sprigs several inches long in water (see earlier conditioning instructions) and insert one, standing straight up, into the top center of the oasis. Then work from top to bottom, turning the tree as you go and progressively increasing the length of the sprigs. Change the angle of the sprigs, too, gradually moving from upright to a downward slope as you reach the bottom of the oasis block. Pack the sprigs together tightly, and trim off any uneven lengths to achieve a smooth, dense coat. Then add roses; you'll need several dozen. A garnish of spring colors and ribbon can make this an Easter tree, while a garland of red roses will suit fall better. Mist the finished tree periodically and keep it well watered. If you replace the roses as they fade, the arrangement should last at least two weeks.

Mock Topiary Trees

For a striking, unusual centerpiece, combine your old roses with an assortment of greens to create a mock topiary tree. Begin again with a block of wet oasis, this time cutting it into a rectangular shape. Mount the block on a dowel that you have previously affixed firmly to a base. One way of achieving this is to sink the base of the dowel into a pot full of wet plaster. Cover the oasis block with assorted, short-stemmed greens, turning it into a dense ball of foliage. Then add roses (you'll need at least two dozen), using blossoms of all colors and sizes and in all stages of bloom from bud to full blown. Once the "tree" is complete, mist it thoroughly. If you plan to place it on the dining table, be sure to make the dowel stem long enough for the ball of foliage and flowers to stand above the guests' eye level when they are seated. Like boxwood trees, the topiary tree is adaptable to a variety of holidays through addition of holiday motifs.

A pittosporum base is covered with roses for a dining room centerpiece. The roses are 'Vanity,' 'Skyrocket,' 'Cramoisi Supérieur,' 'Old Blush,' 'Cécile Brünner,' "Caldwell Pink," and "Gay Hill Red China."

Rose Crafts
Potpourri, Waxed Roses & More

CHAPTER FIVE

Margaret P. Sharpe

IF YOU GROW and show roses long enough (and it may take some years), eventually the extravagance of dead-heading will come to trouble you. Pinching off an old rose's fading blossoms and fruits (the hips or "heps" as they are commonly known) may be essential to the bush's continued bloom, but to discard this colorful, perfumed material seems terribly wasteful—and it is, because those throwaway petals and fruits can be used in so many creative crafts. By combining them with other plant materials—herbs, spices, and annual and perennial flowers—you can transform dead heads into wonderful gifts and art objects. Best of all, this work doesn't require special equipment or any major expenditure of money.

What follows is an introduction to rose crafts. You'll find the recipes included here simple and easy to follow. They are also thoroughly tested, so they'll start you on the path of rose recycling without a stumble. (For a list of sources for rose craft materials, refer to the back of the book.)

This beautifully patterned rose bowl is a creative use of frequently discarded materials.

Wonderful Potpourris

THE most prominent of the rose crafts is also the oldest, since aromatic confections of rose petals, herbs, and spices have been serving as natural air fresheners since the days of the pharaohs. The exact ingredients used by ancient Egyptians remain a mystery, but samples recovered from tombs have sometimes preserved a hint of fragrance even after thousands of years. The techniques employed today are of more recent origin, but still centuries old.

Potpourris fall into two broad classes. The first is the moist potpourri, in which ingredients release their perfume through a sort of fermentation. It is this type that inspired the name potpourri, which means "rotten pot" in French. The other type is the dry potpourri, which uses only thoroughly dried ingredients. Although its fragrance is less intense, it is simpler to make and offers a good introduction to this craft.

Here are some hints for making outstanding potpourris:

- Keep the ingredients away from contact with metal. Use glass, plastic, or glazed containers and wood or plastic utensils. Avoid unnecessary exposure to light.
- When calculating quantities of ingredients, remember that as they dry, rose petals shrink to one-third their original volume.
- If salt is called for, as in moist potpourris, use plain salt with no additives. Salt with additives will destroy the natural chemicals in the rose petals.
- White and pale pink petals turn brown as they dry, and yellow petals may also turn an unattractive color. As a result, these sorts are best suited to wet potpourris, in which the petals are hidden from view.
- Use fragrant rose petals. Roses are at peak fragrance and ideal for potpourri-making when the blooms are only half open. In general, early morning is the best time to cut flowers for this purpose, since the blossoms' perfumes are freshest at that time. There is no single best time of year, however, for peak fragrance.

'Zéphirine Drouhin,'
a thornless climbing
Bourbon Rose, is among
the highly fragrant roses
that grow well in the
South.

Roses for Fragrance

THE Damasks and Centifolias have long been acclaimed the most fragrant of roses, and it is these two classes that fill the fields of commercial perfumeries in France and Bulgaria. There are other classes, however, that are nearly as fragrant and grow far better in the American South. Foremost among these are the Musk Roses and their descendants, the Hybrid Musks and Noisettes. The fragrance of these roses derives primarily from the wild rose, *Rosa moschata*, and this species's spicy scent is recognizable in nearly all the crosses. Though modest in appearance, the wild Musk Rose was prized from an early date because its scent recalled the pleasantly strong fragrance of the musk glands of Asian musk deer, an exotic and costly basis for popular perfumes. While the beauty of this rose and its descendants is certainly not to be discounted, nevertheless it is the fragrance of the wild Musk Rose that has moved poets and charmed suitors, and so won the rose fame.

For specific recommendations of good roses for making potpourri, refer to the list of roses with outstanding fragrance in the appendix.

Effective potpourris, both moist and dry, depend on judicious blending of three types of ingredients: they must have a main scent, blenders, and, most important, fixatives.

Above. Rose petals are the most important main scent for potpourri.
Right. Main scents, blenders, and fixatives are required for all potpourri. Illustrated are (clockwise): rose leaves, rose petals, lavender, rose buds, lemon peel (diced), bay leaves, vanilla beans, stick cinnamon, rosemary leaves, whole cloves, star anise, and orris root.

Main Scents

The first decision to be made in concocting a successful potpourri is the choice of a main scent—the fragrance that will serve as the blend's dominant theme. In a rose potpourri, generally, the main scent is supplied by rose petals. Other ingredients are added to enhance or modify this fragrance, to tune it to a logical consistency.

There are dozens of other flowers that may be used in a potpourri mixture. Experiment with whatever types you find available to arrive at a combination that satisfies your nose. (When making a dry potpourri, remember that only roses, lavender, citrus flowers, and tuberoses hold their scents after drying, so that most other flowers, foliages, seeds or grasses, roots, and woods you may use in dry form serve only for additional color and bulk.)

Blenders

Blenders are the plant materials you use to add richness and diversity to potpourri while also increasing its bulk. You should take care in selecting them to make sure that their fragrances enhance the main scent rather than overwhelming it.

A common source of blenders is the aromatic herbs. The most popular of these is lavender, which is, after roses, the world's favorite potpourri ingredient. Sadly, lavender does not thrive in the South and must be purchased from herbal supply houses. Better adapted to our climate are the mints, such as peppermint, bergamot mint, and spearmint, which all make good herbs for dry potpourris. Bergamot mint, or orange mint as it is sometimes called, is probably the one most often used for this purpose, since it has a fruity aroma that adds much to floral fragrances. (If you are making dry potpourri, be sure to keep the proportion of mint leaves modest, however. Otherwise the finished product may be more reminiscent of a julep than of a flower garden.) Another useful herb that adds fragrance and bulk to a rose petal potpourri is rose geranium. This, too, grows well in the South. Similarly, citrus peels may be added, primarily as a source of color. To prepare them for use in the dry potpourri, cut the peels into half-inch-square pieces.

Another good blending herb is rosemary (*Rosmarinus officinalis*). This hardy, evergreen shrub thrives in a sunny garden, or in a pot on the porch or windowsill. It prefers a well drained soil, and once well rooted it will prove exceptionally drought hardy. In our region its only serious enemy is intense cold. With its clean, penetrating fragrance, rosemary is valuable not only for potpourris but also for sachets.

Thyme, marjoram, and basil are also used in potpourri and can be grown easily in home gardens. Patchouli is still another herb sometimes used in potpourri. It has a powerful, somewhat strange aroma. Lemon verbena is another favorite of Southern gardeners, although it is perennial only in Zones 9 and 10—the extreme southern and coastal portions of the South.

Ordinary culinary spices also work well as blenders in potpourris. Those most commonly employed for this purpose are cloves, cinnamon, and nutmeg. Though these can be used if crushed or ground, the whole spices are preferable because they keep their scents longer. Other ingredients from the spice rack suitable for dry potpourri include vanilla beans and seed of dill, fennel, caraway, and coriander; these last can be harvested directly from the garden. Various woods can also add interesting scents, textures, and color to dry potpourris. Many recipes call for sandalwood. Its sweet, woody fragrance is a perfect complement to the scent of roses.

Whichever of these materials you may choose, keep in mind that the keys to their successful incorporation into a potpourri are careful selection of types, and moderation in the amount you add.

Potpourri ingredients prior to mixing: gomphrena, rose petals, cedar shavings, rose leaves, lavender, statice (center), and star anise on a bed of rosemary leaves

Brightly-colored and uniquely-shaped seeds, seed heads, and flowers are
good candidates for potpourris.

Fixatives

THESE are ingredients that, by stabilizing the perfumes, give the potpourri a long life. Fixatives are essential to both wet and dry blends, for without them, the various materials quickly expend their fragrance into the atmosphere. Undoubtedly the most widely used of all fixatives is the dried root of the Florentine iris, called orris root. Other plant materials that can serve this purpose are lemon grass, oakmoss, reindeer moss, gum benzoin, balsam, frankincense, myrrh, and vetiver. All can be purchased from herbal supply houses.

There are also a number of animal essences used as fixatives, possibly the best known being musk. By far the most powerful scent used in perfumery, musk is generally available in tinctures (that is, dissolved in alcohol solvents) and is effective even in very small amounts. Two other animal essences are ambergris and civet, which are also sold as tinctures. All of these are expensive, but they add greatly to the life and fragrance of any potpourri product. Plan to add at least one to any collection of potpourri materials.

A final note on ingredients: if you are making a dry potpourri, you must thoroughly dehydrate all the leaves of herbs and spices before adding them to the blend, so that they will not later mildew or mold. The simplest and most effective method for accomplishing this is to wash the leaves, pat them dry with a paper towel, and then place them in a paper grocery bag. Fold the top of the bag over a few times and clip it shut with a clothespin. Allow time for the leaves to dry to a paper crispness, perhaps two to three weeks in humid atmospheres and ten days in a dry climate.

The advantage of this technique is that it preserves the color of the leaves as well as the fragrance. Some people use a microwave oven for drying, and others place the leaves on a tray in a regular oven. However, by using heat to dry herbs and spices, you run the risk of destroying the essential oils that are the source of their fragrances.

Moist Potpourris

OF rose potpourri Gertrude Jekyll, one of the most revered garden designers of the twentieth century, once said, "The dry is much the easier and quicker to make, but is neither so sweet nor so enduring, so now the moist is the only kind I care to have."

In making a moist potpourri, the rose petals are dried only partially so that they retain most of their beautifully scented natural oils. This produces a blend that is both longer lasting and stronger smelling than the dry mixtures. However, making a moist potpourri takes from several weeks to an entire summer, so it is a project only for someone with patience and perseverance.

The moist method is the oldest way of making potpourri, and consequently there are many recipes. Practically speaking, however, there are only two steps to keep in mind. The first is that of mixing wilted, or half dried, rose petals with plain salt and allowing them to ferment. The second is adding herbs and spices and letting the mixture mellow, or "cure." A list of materials needed, aside from the ingredients of the chosen recipe, includes:

- A wide-mouthed, straight-sided container of glazed pottery, glass, or plastic and a cover or lid (a one-gallon size is excellent)
- A long-handled wooden or plastic spoon for mixing the ingredients
- A heavy dish or saucer slightly smaller than the inside circumference of the container (weighted down with a heavy rock or small brick, this compresses the ingredients as they ferment)
- Medium ground or coarse non-iodized salt
- A drying frame with fabric netting or plastic screening, or old newspapers
- Containers to hold the prepared potpourri

Mixing the Ingredients

U SE roses and flowers that are fresh and highly fragrant. Remove the petals and spread them in a single layer over a drying frame or screen, or on newspaper. Place in a dark, well ventilated place such as an attic, under a bed, or on a closet shelf. When the petals become limp and have a somewhat leathery feel (after two or three days), they have dried to the proper stage.

At that point, layer about one quart of petals inside the one-gallon, straight-sided container, and sprinkle a heaping tablespoon of salt evenly over them. Then add another quart of petals and another tablespoon of salt, and continue alternating the two until you have filled the container. You may do this all at once or gradually over a period of several weeks if your source of rose petals is limited. In either case, when you finish adding material (even if only temporarily), weight it down with the saucer and stone. By compressing the layers of petals and salt, you cause them to cake together. Cover the container with a lid and store it on an easily reached shelf in a dry place. Once a day, remove the cover, dish, and weight, and stir the mixture, scraping any residue off the sides of the container.

Curing the Mixture

WHEN the petals have formed a dense mass, usually after two to three weeks, add the fixatives, blenders, scented herbs and spices, and essential oils that are called for in the recipe you have chosen.

At this stage the potpourri may smell "raw," but it will improve as it ages. When flowers begin to dry they have a marvelous aroma, but when they are halfway dry, they smell as though they should be thrown out. After the potpourri has matured, or aged, the raw odor will leave, and the original floral odor will return. So replace the mass of ingredients in the original curing container, weight it, cover it, and put the container back in the closet for at least six weeks to age and mellow into wonderful potpourri.

The Old-Fashioned Rose Jar

DURING the curing period, keep yourself busy with a search for appropriate, decorative containers. Moist potpourri must be kept in a container with a lid (preferably one pierced by little holes) so that you can enjoy its fragrance without looking at the unattractive stew of dark brown ingredients. The best containers of all are the old-fashioned rose jars that were made specifically for this purpose. They are similar to oriental ginger jars, except that the rose jars have two lids; one is pierced by holes so that the fragrance can waft forth and the other is a solid cap to cover and close the jar. This extra cap, incidentally, is important, because a moist potpourri must be prevented from drying out if it is to keep its fragrance. Stories you may have heard about "feeding Grandma's rose jar every year" suggest how long such a potpourri may hold its fragrance if kept moist and rejuvenated periodically with the addition of a few extremely fragrant rose petals or a few drops of essential oils. The addition of a little alcohol will also enhance a faded fragrance.

Moist potpourri displayed with one container lid removed

Knole House Moist Potpourri

T̲H̲I̲S̲ moist potpourri comes from Vita Sackville-West's birthplace. Layer the following with 1/4 pound of coarse, non-iodized salt: 7 quarts of partially dried ingredients—rose petals, lavender flowers, lemon balm, lemon verbena leaves, rosemary, violets, and rose geranium leaves.

For the spice mixture blend the following:

1 teaspoon each powdered cinnamon, powdered mace, powdered nutmeg, and cut lemon peel
1 tablespoon powdered orris root (fixative)
1 1/2 teaspoons powdered gum benzoin

Follow the procedure for making moist potpourri. Let the initial petal mixture cure, add the spice mixture, and age to maximum fragrance. This should make about one quart of cured and aged potpourri.

Dry Potpourris

PRESENT day rose bowls, or dry potpourris, incorporate not only rose petals, but also many unperfumed flowers, brightly colored and uniquely shaped seeds and seed heads, and even slices of dried exotic fruits. In addition to floral perfumes, such blends may also furnish fruity, oriental, and woodsy aromas. In contrast to traditional potpourris, modern ones depend less on the fragrances of flowers, herbs, and spices, since the wide availability of essential oils today makes it a simple matter to reinforce a dry mixture's fragrance. Their ease of preparation makes dry potpourris more suitable to a modern lifestyle than the more laborious and time-consuming moist potpourris. Yet another advantage of the dry mixture is that almost any container will serve; these potpourris can be set out in antique wooden bowls, shells, or baskets, or kept in sachets in lace, embroidery, or cutwork bags.

Simple Rose Potpourri

2 cups dried rose petals, medium pink to medium red, and some bright yellows or blends of yellow, pink, and rose
1 tablespoon *crushed* orris root or cedar wood chips (fixative)
1 tablespoon broken cloves
1 tablespoon broken cinnamon
3 torn bay laurel leaves (*Laurus nobilis*)

Stir in: 10 drops rose oil
       3 to 5 drops lemon oil
       10 drops ambergris (fixative)

Mix the ingredients well in a plastic or ceramic bowl, and stir in the oils. Try to choose a day when the humidity is low to do this so that the petals won't soften. Funnel the resulting mixture into a large glass jar with an airtight lid and seal it. Shake every three to four days, keeping the jar at room temperature. It should be ready in about a month.

Note: Powdered spices and orris root should not be used in making dry potpourris since they give the petals an unattractive, dusty appearance.

Traditional rose bowl

Traditional Rose Bowl

1 quart dried rose petals, buds, and blooms
1 cup dried fragrant rose leaves
2 ounces dried lemon verbena leaves
1 ounce lavender
2 teaspoons broken cinnamon
1/2 teaspoon whole cloves
2 tablespoons crushed orris root (fixative)
5 drops rose oil
2 drops lavender oil
1 drop patchouli oil, if desired

Mix and age as for previous recipe. (For the fragrant leaves called for here, use any from the Moss Roses, or 'Eglantine,' the leaves of which have a lovely apple scent.)

An olive twig basket with
piquant potpourri

Piquant Potpourri

1 quart dried rose petals of medium pinks through deep reds
2 ounces lemon balm and lemon verbena dried leaves
1 ounce lavender (2 tablespoons)
1 ounce dried lemon geranium leaves
1 ounce dried rosemary
1/4 lemon rind, diced and dried
1 ounce crushed orris root (fixative)
1 teaspoon crushed cinnamon
1 teaspoon broken cloves
3 drops lemon oil
1 drop each of rose and lavender oil.

Mix and age as for recipe above.

Whole rose stems are easily dried by hanging them upside down.

Drying Roses

THIS is an essential preliminary to making potpourris, but blossoms preserved in this fashion also make an elegant addition to all sorts of dried arrangements and will extend the pleasure of roses right through winter's frost and summer's drought. Several methods for drying roses will be described here, but of these, the most popular is air drying. This slow, relatively gentle process poses the least risk of depleting the oils that give rose petals their fragrance, and, if done in a dark location, it leaves the colors more or less intact. Finally, air drying permits the preservation of whole roses, stems and all, if the flowers are tied in bunches and hung upside down. Air drying does not work well with large blossoms, however, since their buds hold so much moisture that they mold before they dry. No method of drying is entirely satisfactory for the biggest roses.

Each tussie mussie bouquet is hand-tied with burgundy ribbon and includes small crystal cones filled with rose potpourri.

Air Drying Petals

For making dry potpourris, you must preserve the petals loose rather than in whole flowers. To accomplish this, you need only set them on drying screens in a well ventilated location. They should be easily accessible, though, since the petals will require daily attention as they dry. Any square or rectangular frame, like a window screen frame, makes a good drying screen. You can also make one yourself by stretching screening over a frame made of two six-foot-long, 1″ × 2″ wooden strips. Whichever frames you use, you must make provision to support them above the floor so that air can circulate all around the petals. A well ventilated attic makes an ideal place, in that warmth promotes rapid drying, while darkness will protect the petals' color.

Left. A large fir tree trimmed with thousands of twinkle lights and hundreds of tussie mussies composed of dried roses and other garden flowers is the focal point of the State Drawing Room in the Georgia's Governor's Mansion.

Spread the petals over the drying screen in a single layer, making sure that they do not overlap and stick together. During the first two or three days, stir and turn the petals about three times daily to assure even, mold-free drying. As the drying progresses, the need for stirring decreases; eventually the petals will become as crisp as cornflakes. At this stage you may store them in a heavy plastic bag, or in a plastic bucket with an airtight lid, until needed. It is important that the petals be kept in the dark to prevent the color from fading.

Because of the relatively mild climate in the South it is almost inevitable that some insect eggs will lie hidden among rose petals collected at any time of year. Sometime after you've finished a dry potpourri, you may notice that holes are appearing in the dried petals, and a fine powder collecting in the container. This is evidence that your hitchhikers have hatched and are beginning to feed. An effective solution to this problem (although, admittedly, not an ideal one) is to add a teaspoon of 5% Sevin powder (carboryl) to each gallon of dry petals as you put them in a plastic bag for storage. Shake the sealed bag well to distribute the powder over the petals thoroughly.

Silica Gel Drying

If you want your roses to keep their color, by far the best method of drying them is to bury them in silica gel. White and granular, silica gel looks much like sugar, except that scattered throughout it are small blue particles. It is a universal drying agent and may be purchased from any source of floral supplies. When the silica gel begins to turn pink, it is full of moisture and must be dried out in a conventional oven (on low temperature for an hour) or in a microwave. To keep it from absorbing atmospheric humidity, silica gel should be stored in an airtight container; for the same reason, whenever you use it to dry flowers, you should do so in an environment low in humidity.

Selecting blossoms at the proper stage of maturity is essential when working with silica gel. Choose roses that are one-half to two-thirds open and full of moisture. This last requirement may seem like a disadvantage, but in fact it helps to ensure that the petals remain securely attached and at the peak of their colors. Even so, you will find that roses change their colors as they dry, but you'll soon learn which ones you prefer. As a rule, dark reds turn black, and orange-reds turn red. Pink roses darken in hue, and yellows usually fade, while white roses turn a dingy tan or parchment color. Probably the roses least affected are the light rose-reds.

Petals should be dried on a drying screen.

The silica gel method of drying best maintains the natural flower colors.

Prepare the roses for drying by cutting the stems to within one inch of the calyx. Pour silica gel over the bottom of the drying container to a depth of an inch, set the roses face up in this, and push their stubs of stems down to the bottom of the container. Make sure that no rose touches another. Using a small scoop and your fingers, gently pour silica gel under, around, and between all the petals, taking care that petals do not become misshapen and that gel touches all parts of the bloom. Completely cover each bloom with silica gel in this manner. Then seal the top of the drying container and label it with the current date and the date you plan to open it. Roses usually require four to five days in silica gel to dry.

At the completion of that period, open the container in a very dry location and gently tilt it, pouring enough of the gel into another container to allow you to see the tops of the flowers. Gently slip two fingers into the gel under one of the blooms. Lift the blossom slowly above the gel, tilting and turning it to clear it of gel as best you can. Feel the calyx: if it is hard and crisp, the drying process is complete. Dust off any remnants of gel with a fine watercolor brush, set the rose aside, and move on to the next flower in the container.

Microwave Drying

Basically, this method is the same as the preceding one, except that, by "cooking" the flowers and gel in a microwave oven, you can shorten the drying period from days to minutes. Gather and prepare the roses just as you did before, but put them and the gel in a microwave-safe, sturdy cardboard shoe box.

After arranging the roses and gel in the shoe box, center it, uncovered, on the turntable of a 600W microwave oven. Set the oven's controls to low, and turn it on for fifteen minutes. After the oven turns itself off, leave it closed for at least thirty minutes, because the roses will have become quite fragile and should be left to cool gradually and without disturbance. When you do open the oven, if you find the roses less than completely dry, replace them in the silica gel and return them to the oven. Set the controls to low again, but heat this time for just two or three minutes. Repeat, if necessary, until the roses emerge well dried but not brittle. Heating rose petals can change the chemistry of their fragrant oils, so do not expect much fragrance from a rose bloom dried by heating.

Selected Rose Crafts

Rose Wreaths

Making a wreath of dried roses can be a delightful project. First you'll have to assemble a supply of dried roses and other flowers. Then you'll have to wire the flowers so that you can stick them into a foam or straw base. To give the wreath a full effect, make sure to use a generous quantity of flowers so that you cover the form completely.

Rose Petal Figurines

Beautiful and pleasantly scented art objects may be created by covering small figurines and baskets with crumbled, dried rose petals or potpourri. Animal figures are readily available at craft shops, some covered with a suedelike coating and some of smooth ceramic. To coat these, or small, finely woven baskets, have rose petals dried to cornflake crispness.

A potpourri of rose crafts

Above. A potpourri-covered basket
Right. Dried roses, rose buds, globe amaranth,
cockscomb, hydrangea, and peonies adorn
a wreath at the Georgia Governor's Mansion.
Magnolia, ivy, beech leaves, fresh rosemary,
and lavender provide greenery.

Dry potpourri may also be used. Crumble the potpourri or petals to a size appropriate to the scale of the object you are covering. To achieve a very fine texture, process the dried petals or potpourri in a blender for a few seconds.

Coat part of the object with plain white glue, using generous brushfuls. Roll the glue-covered part of the figure in the crushed petals or potpourri, lightly pressing on additional dried material until no more will adhere.

If a figure loses color after a while, it may be refreshed by applying an additional coating. And the fragrance may be enhanced on a potpourri coating by lightly spraying on some rose or other cologne.

The Art of Waxing Rose Blooms

WAXING roses was a popular method of preservation from the Victorian era on into the early twentieth century. If the practitioner were adept, the waxed blooms could scarcely be distinguished from fresh ones. It's still a great way to preserve roses and make them last from one to three months.

Assemble the following:

conditioned, refrigerated roses
1-quart clean, empty can
2-quart saucepan
12 cakes (3 pounds) paraffin
candy thermometer
#20–#22 florist wire
wire cutters
empty pop bottles
supply of old newspapers
cardboard box no smaller than 12″ × 18″ × 12″

Spread newspapers over the floor where you will be working to protect it from spattered paraffin. Put the paraffin in the 1-quart can, and set it in the saucepan. Fill the saucepan with water until the can of paraffin starts to float. Heat slowly to warm the wax. *Never heat wax over direct heat.*

Just before the paraffin finishes melting, remove about six rose blooms from the refrigerator. Cut stems to about two inches, and create an artificial stem of #20 or #22 florist wire by piercing the wire through the calyx. Stand each one in a bottle to await waxing.

Refrigerating the roses serves not only to keep them fresh but also to protect them from the heat of the wax. Though paraffin must reach 140° before it melts, a temperature of just 115° destroys the cell structure of rose petals. Even with thorough chilling, a rose can stand only the briefest exposure to the paraffin, so you must work quickly and surely.

Carefully watch the paraffin melting in the can. As soon as it turns liquid and clear, check the temperature with a candy thermometer. If it is hotter than 140°, remove the can from the hot water and let it cool down to that point. Then, holding a rose by the bottom end of its wire stem, quickly dip it into the paraffin, briefly swirling the blossom around in the hot liquid. As soon as the rose is covered, immediately remove it and shake off any excess wax into the cardboard box with a slinging, downward motion. Do not try to redip the rose. Stand the wire stem in the bottle again so that the wax may harden undisturbed. When cool, the treated bloom will be fragile, but it will hold its color for a week to a month. It will keep its form for many months, so that even after it has faded, the waxed rose may be spray painted for other decorative uses. Silver- or gold-sprayed waxed roses are especially useful at Christmastime; they make beautiful and unusual wreaths or table decorations.

Rose Beads

Assemble the following:

45 to 50 rose hips
heavy nylon thread
2 pounds silica gel or borax

Collect large, bright red hips, taking them all from the same rose variety so that they are uniform in shape. Wash and dry them, and set them aside. Pour about one inch of dessicant (either silica gel or borax) into the bottom of an airtight container with a tightly fitting lid. Then spread a layer of hips over the dessicant, spacing them an inch or so apart. Cover with another inch of dessicant, and spread another layer of hips, continuing until you fill the container or until you use up all your hips. Cover the container tightly, and leave it to dry for about ten days. Hips dry slowly since they are large and full of live seeds, so don't try to hurry the process.

Once the hips have dried, you may string them without further preparation. Grip each one with a pair of pliers and carefully drill a hole through the hip's exact center. An electric drill with a one-sixteenth-inch bit works best. You may want to bore holes in a number of large, dried rose seeds, too, since alternating these with the hips will give the finished string of beads more flexibility. Once you've arranged the beads to your satisfaction, thread them onto a length of heavy nylon string. The old style of braided fishing line, if available, is best; modern monofilament fishing line is a little too stiff to allow the beads to fall naturally.

Do not put any protective coating on rose hip beads. These coatings cause color changes in the hips that often look unnatural, and the smell of solvents may linger a long time. The best way to protect beads is to store them, when not in use, in a tightly closed plastic bag. For additional protection, once a year drop a pinch of 5% Sevin dust into the bag. This discourages any insects that might otherwise attack your homegrown jewelry.

Candied Rose Petals

Candied rose petals receive a coating of egg white prior to being dipped in powdered sugar.

Assemble the following:

Large, clean rose petals, not whites or dark reds (**Important:** Be sure petals have never been treated with systemic insecticides)
1 egg white, slightly beaten
powdered sugar
2 small saucers
tweezers, waxed paper, tray, watercolor brush

Clean petals by rinsing them well. Spread them out on a paper towel and blot them dry with a tissue. Place the egg white in a saucer with low sides; do the same with the powdered sugar. With a watercolor brush, paint each petal on both sides with the egg white. Then, with a pair of tweezers, pick up the egg-white-saturated petals and drop them one at a time into the powdered sugar. Turn the petals with the tweezers several times to coat both sides with sugar, so that they have a frosted appearance. Lay the well-coated petals on a piece of waxed paper, and set them in a dark, dry location. Check daily and turn any that seem slow about drying on the bottom. In about three days, they should become dry and crisp.

Rose Hip Jam

Assemble the following:

1 pint clean and juicy rose hips
(**Important:** Be sure that the hips have never been treated with systemic insecticides)
1 pint water
2 tart apples
2 1/4 cups sugar (1 pound)
2 tablespoons lemon juice

Cook the rose hips and apples in the water until very tender. Puree the resulting mixture by forcing it through a sieve. Add sugar and lemon juice. Bring to a rolling boil for 10 to 15 minutes, until the jam thickens. Pour immediately into sterile, hot glasses or jars. Let cool, and seal with jar lid or pour paraffin on top. Makes 16 ounces.

Rose Petal Jelly

Assemble the following:

2 quarts fresh rose petals, heels removed
4 cups water
3/4 cup sugar
1 package jelling mix
1 teaspoon lemon juice

Boil water and add rose petals. Steep 3 to 5 minutes and strain. Reboil rose water, and add the sugar and jelling mix. Boil 1 minute, stirring constantly. Remove from heat and add lemon juice. Skim off any foam and pour immediately into hot, sterile glasses. Leave 1/2 inch of space at top for paraffin seal.

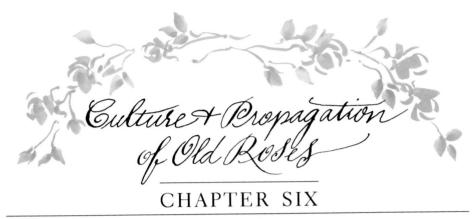

Culture & Propagation of Old Roses

CHAPTER SIX
Rose Culture

Roses are amazingly versatile plants that respond favorably to a wide variety of growing conditions. A number of gardening practices help produce healthy plants and prolific blooming. The most important of these are good site selection, soil preparation, proper planting, application of fertilizers, treatment for insects and diseases, watering, and pruning.

Sites and Soils

Roses are sturdier and produce more flowers in full or nearly full sun, so choose a site with at least five or six hours of direct sun each day. Early morning sun is especially desirable since it quickly dries any moisture on the plants, thus reducing disease problems.

Good drainage is essential for all but a few varieties of roses. If water tends to stand in the root zone for extended periods, either choose another location

Left. Rooting hormone, cuttings ready for rooting, and rooted cuttings

or raise the planting bed enough to improve the drainage. Consider the site's air circulation as well. Good air circulation helps prevent diseases, but extremely windy sites may require windbreak protection for good flower and foliage quality.

Roses can thrive in a wide variety of soils, although some soils may require modification. Clay soils are preferable and can be improved by incorporating four to six inches of compost, pine bark, peat moss, or similar organic material into the upper foot of soil. Agricultural gypsum mixed into heavy, alkaline clay can also improve soil texture. Sandy soils require even larger amounts of organic material to help hold the water and nutrients necessary for good growth and flowering.

Roses prefer a slightly acid soil (pH 6.0–6.8). Soil pH can usually be raised about one point by adding five pounds of ground limestone per hundred square feet of soil area. To lower pH or to make the soil more acid, incorporate three pounds of iron sulfate or one pound of ground sulfur per hundred square feet. Soil preparation can be done immediately prior to planting but is more effective if completed several months before. Earlier preparation facilitates the plant's absorption of organic materials and nutrients.

Planting

ALLOW for proper spacing of your antique roses before planting. Spacing of the plants will differ with varieties. Some Polyanthas can be planted as close together as eighteen inches, while Chinas, Bourbons, Teas, Hybrid Perpetuals, Hybrid Teas, and Hybrid Musks flourish at three to five feet apart, depending on the variety. Climbers and ramblers need more space to develop their potential. Eight to ten feet is appropriate for most, but under good conditions Banksias, 'Cherokee,' and certain others could be spaced at intervals of fifteen feet or more.

Bare root plants should be set out as soon after receiving them as weather and time allow. If a delay of more than a few days is necessary, remove the plants from the shipping bag and "heel them in" by covering the roots and part of the top with loose soil. Container-grown plants may be set out at any time, but most rose growers avoid the hot summer months, when extra irrigation and care may be necessary to ensure success.

Prune tops back an inch or two, cutting just above a live and healthy bud on each cane. Trim back to healthy tissue any canes or roots damaged in shipping or handling.

To plant only a few roses, dig individual holes for them. These holes should be at least twelve inches deep and eighteen inches wide—large enough to accommodate the natural spread of the roots. Mix about one-third organic material (peat, pine bark, or compost) with some of the soil from the hole, along with a gallon or two of well-rotted cow manure, if available, to fill the hole. A half-cup of bone meal or superphosphate thoroughly mixed with the soil is also a good idea. A similar amount of agricultural gypsum is beneficial for heavy alkaline clay soils. Pack the soil firmly around the roots and water thoroughly to remove air pockets and settle the soil. Plants should be set at approximately the same level at which they have been growing or slightly deeper.

Fertilizing

Roses are heavy users of nutrients and respond favorably to the frequent application of fertilizers. To determine fertility of existing soil, it is a good idea to contact your county extension agent for instructions on submitting a soil sample.

For everblooming types, fertilizers should not be applied until the first set of flowers begins to fade; in the case of once-blooming roses, eight to ten weeks after planting. A heaping tablespoon per plant of a complete fertilizer such as 6–10–4 or 8–8–8 may be applied every four to six weeks until about two months prior to the average date of first frost. Application after that time can promote soft fall growth that may result in freeze damage.

The time-honored fertilizer and soil conditioner for roses is well-rotted cow manure. Since manure is often unavailable today, however, commercial fertilizers have become popular. Phosphorous is the material that helps plants develop strong, healthy roots and prolific flowering. Superphosphate is usually available and can be applied at the rate of three to four pounds per hundred square feet. Since phosphorous is not very mobile in the soil, it should be well mixed during preparation.

Nitrogen is easily and quickly depleted from the soil and needs to be applied periodically during the growing season. It is necessary for more and bigger canes, stems, and leaves. Potassium is needed for promotion of new growth, disease resistance, and cold tolerance. All three nutrients (nitrogen, phosphorous, and potassium) are included in balanced fertilizers, which many rose growers apply every four to six weeks through the growing season.

Watering

WHILE most modern roses require watering, many antique roses are drought resistant and can exist on rainfall alone in much of the South once established. Yet supplemental irrigation is also recommended for old roses in order to encourage more attractive plants and much greater volume and quality of blossoms. Water can be applied efficiently with soaker hoses, drip irrigation, or specially designed automatic sprinkling devices, keeping in mind that most rose varieties are less disease prone if their foliage remains dry. Deep watering at weekly intervals is far superior to frequent light sprinkling.

Mulches can help conserve water while moderating soil temperatures during extremely hot weather. It is an excellent practice to apply a layer several inches thick of bark, pine needles, or even coastal Bermuda grass hay to beds or individual plants. The mulch can be supplemented with well-rotted cow manure during the winter, thus adding organic material as well as some fertility to the soil.

Insects and Diseases

SOME gardeners choose to grow old roses because they are often more resistant to insect and disease problems, but this resistance varies considerably among varieties. Roses grown in open, sunny areas with good air circulation tend to be freer of such pests.

Insecticides such as Malathion, Diazinon, or Orthene can be effective in controlling aphids, thrips, and other insect pests. Miticides are used to control spider mites. Insecticidal soaps are also becoming popular and are effective in controlling mites and many other insects.

The major problem for roses in most of the South is a fungal disease called black spot. If left unchecked on susceptible varieties, black spot can cause plants to lose most of their leaves. The disease appears as circular black spots frequently surrounded by a yellow halo. Infected leaves yellow and drop off prematurely. Benomyul, Funginex, or Maneb used according to label instructions are effective in the control of black spot disease.

Powdery mildew is another diseases that attacks some varieties, especially in the spring and fall. It appears as white powdery spores, similar in appearance to flour, on young shoots and buds and can cause distortion of foliage and flowers. Materials such as Funginex applied according to label instructions usually control the problem.

Pruning

THE traditional heavy pruning practices may be appropriate for Hybrid Teas, but most old roses require less severe methods. Diseased or dead canes should be removed or cut back to healthy tissue any time during the year. General thinning of weak or crowded growth can best be accomplished in February or early March in most of Texas and the South. Shaping the plants and shortening the vigorous canes by one-fourth to one-third of their length can result in more attractive plants. Care should be taken to prune most climbers and one-time bloomers *after* they flower in the spring so as not to reduce their seasonal show.

Keep in mind that most old garden roses are attractive landscape plants with a pleasing natural form, a form which should still be apparent after pruning. In addition to late-winter pruning, some rosarians cut their plants back moderately in mid-August. This practice, along with a light application of fertilizer and a thorough watering, if needed, can promote an excellent fall floral display in many varieties.

Hybrid Teas, Floribundas, and Grandifloras are usually pruned heavily in late winter (down to eighteen to twenty-four inches from the ground). Miniatures are pruned to a few inches above the ground at that time.

Cutting Flowers

IMPROPER cutting of flowers can injure the plant and decrease its vigor. It is best to cut few, if any, flowers during the first blooming season after planting. By removing only flowers and not stems, you will encourage plants to develop into larger bushes by fall, at which time some flowers and stems may be cut. Early removal of flowers with foliage and long stems reduces the food manufacturing capacity of the plant and subsequent bloom yield.

When cutting, use sharp tools and allow at least two leaves to remain between the cut and the main stem. Use sharp shears or a knife and cut the stem immediately above the topmost leaf. Roses that are cut just before the petals begin to unfold will open normally and remain in good condition longer. Late afternoon is the best time of day to cut roses (unless you are cutting in the morning either to condition your roses for arranging or to get the most fragrance for potpourri). For more information on extending the life of cut roses refer to chapter four "Arranging Old Roses."

Propagating Roses from Cuttings

ONE of the joys of growing antique roses is the fact that most of them thrive as own-root plants; that is, they will grow as well—or better—from cuttings as when grafted onto a rootstock the way most modern roses are grown and sold. Rooting cuttings is a relatively simple matter. It is the way most old roses were handed down from one family member or friend to another, and the way many old rose collectors prefer growing them today. Fortunately for us in Texas and the South, most of our better adapted old roses are particularly well suited to growing on their own roots and can be propagated successfully by anyone interested in making the effort. Remember that roses still under patent (seventeen years from date of introduction) cannot legally be propagated without paying a royalty to the holder of the patent.

Some old roses, like those in the Gallica and Rugosa classes, tend to sucker badly and may spread into areas where they are not welcome. If this is a concern, varieties that sucker may be grafted or budded onto a rootstock that does not have this characteristic, such as 'Fortuniana,' *Rosa multiflora*, or 'Dr. Huey.'

The following suggestions for rooting rose cuttings are not likely to result in ninety to one hundred percent rooting, but neither do they require special structures, watering systems, or daily supervision. Success will vary because of the large number of variables involved, but many people report that fifty to seventy-five percent of the cuttings they treat in this manner develop into usable plants.

Taking and Preparing Cuttings

ROSES may be rooted at any time of the year but, for home gardeners, success is much more likely during the cool months from November through February. Late fall is a favorite time because there are usually a few blossoms still remaining on everblooming types to identify them.

The easiest part of the rose to root is the tip of a stem that has recently bloomed. Ideally, these tips have withered flowers or hips beginning to form. The flower heads or hips should be removed down to the first set of healthy leaves. Cuttings should be six to eight inches long and should be cut from the parent plant with a sharp knife or pruning shears at an angle of

This specimen of 'Harison's Yellow' growing wild is a good source of cuttings.

about forty-five degrees. It is important that the cuttings not be allowed to dry out and that they be protected from extreme heat or cold. Experienced antique rose collectors often carry ice chests, plastic bags, a small amount of water, and ice if they are likely to be in very hot conditions before getting the cuttings to the rooting area. Even a few minutes of exposure to heat, cold, or dry air can endanger a cutting. Cuttings may be stored for several days in this manner, if necessary, but the sooner they are stuck, the better.

The use of rooting hormones has been shown to increase the percentage of cuttings that root and the number of roots per cutting, but it is not necessary for success. Materials such as Rootone are commercially available in powder form and are popular with some rose growers. Others also like to use a concoction called "willow water." Willow water is created by taking approximately one-inch sections of cut branches from willows, splitting them and setting them to soak in a pan of water that has been brought to a rolling boil. (Rain water is ideal.) Allow the willow pieces to steep in the water overnight. It should look like weak tea. Remove the willow pieces and soak the bases of the rose cuttings in the concoction for several hours, or overnight. It is helpful to recut the rose cuttings about a half-inch from the ends before placing them in the willow water.

Willow water may be prepared in advance to facilitate the process. It may also be used for the initial watering of newly stuck cuttings. Although all this sounds a bit far out, research at the Ohio Agricultural Research and Development Center has shown that willows (apparently any species of *Salix*) contain substances that can induce rooting. These substances can be removed from the willow wood by the method described and have been shown in controlled experiments to improve the percentage of cuttings that root.

Locations for Sticking Cuttings

SELECTING the site for sticking the cuttings is very important. Roses prefer a sunny location, but for rooting purposes it is usually best that they be shielded from hot afternoon sun. Bright light—but not direct sunlight—is ideal. It is helpful if the soil is sandy and well drained, and a drip from the roof helps to keep the area moist. An east- or north-facing flower bed against a house or other structure is usually a good choice. The sand or sandy soil should be amended with one-fourth to one-third peat moss, composted pine bark, or similar material. The cutting bed should be well tilled or spaded to insure a good blend of soil and organic materials.

Before sticking the cuttings (setting them into the cutting bed), remove all foliage from their lower halves, but leave that of the upper halves in place. If a powdered hormone is to be used, this is the time to apply it. Tip some of the hormone compound from its container onto a sheet of paper and roll or dip into it the basal end of each cutting. After treatment, tap the cuttings lightly to shake off any loose powder. Use a wooden pencil or dibble to make a

Rooted plant ready to set out

hole for each individual cutting, since this will protect the cutting from damage as it is stuck, and should prevent removal of the rooting hormone. Cuttings should be stuck several inches deep or about half the length of each cutting into the bed, and placed six to eight inches apart in rows. Label each row with a permanent marker stating the variety, if known, or the site where collected, and include the date on which the cuttings were stuck. Be sure to pack the soil firmly around each cutting and water thoroughly.

Care During Rooting

I T is especially important early in the rooting period that the cuttings not be allowed to dry out. This may require watering every other day or so if rain does not occur. Our ancestors often placed a fruit jar over each cutting to keep the humidity high. This is a good practice if someone is there to remove the jar during very sunny or hot weather. It should not be necessary to provide cold protection to the rooting cuttings in most of the South, but extreme cold can cause damage that could be prevented by covering for a few hours or days.

During the first month or two after being stuck, cuttings begin to develop a swelling at the base where roots are to develop, called callus tissue. As the winter yields to spring, the cuttings will sprout roots and new growth. This is a critical time for the new plants and again it is important that they not be allowed to dry out. Although the young plants are usually well rooted by late April or May, it is best to leave them in place until fall or winter. They are extremely vulnerable to stress the first summer and should be allowed to develop a good root system, undisturbed.

Transplanting to a Permanent Location

B Y late fall or winter, the young plants should be ready to move to a permanent location in the landscape. They will be small, but most varieties grow quickly and will produce a fair quantity of flowers by the following spring. To protect them from wind damage, it is usually a good idea to prune back any tall shoots and thin the plants as needed at the time they are being transplanted. During their naturally dormant period in late winter, the plants may be dug either with a ball of soil or bare root. For best results, plant in well-prepared soil in locations receiving at least a half-day of sun. A regular fertilizer program may be started by mid-spring.

Antique Roses for Southern Gardens

CHAPTER SEVEN

I<small>T HAS BEEN</small> estimated that more than ten thousand rose varieties were introduced in the period between 1804 and 1935. This, coupled with the fact that roses can and do frequently mutate (sport), helps us to understand how difficult it can be to identify the roses we find growing in old cemeteries and gardens. Only a fraction of the thousands of varieties introduced are still in commerce today. Of these, even fewer are well adapted to growing conditions in the South.

Although the roses described here are certainly not the only ones for our gardens, they form a unique collection. Most of them have been found by old rose collectors on Southern sites, and have proven their worth by braving the elements and earning the love and respect of generations of gardeners. Others have been mentioned in historical writings about gardens in our part of the country. The remaining varieties have all been tried in Southern gardens and

An antique crock holds an opulent mass of old roses on a farmhouse porch.

found to be worthy of recommendation by experienced old rose aficionados. It is an eclectic group coming from many classes, but by far the largest percentage of antique roses found on old sites are in the Tea and China classes.

Roses are usually divided into classes that might be compared to breeds of animals. Each class has certain general characteristics of foliage, prickles, fragrance, flowers, fruit, and overall size. Some of the best classes have virtually been abandoned by the nursery trade primarily because they are not sufficiently cold hardy to survive in northern climates, where most roses are shipped today. Fortunately for those of us in the South, some of the best of these less cold hardy roses are coming back into production and are once again available to us, even if on a limited scale. (Refer to the list of mail order sources at the end of this chapter.)

Old Roses in the Gulf South

A RECENT popularity poll of old roses was conducted by Mr. and Mrs. Marion L. Brandes, Jr., of Huffman, Texas. Subscribers to *The Old Texas Rose* newsletter were invited to list their five favorite roses in numerous categories. The thirteen participants were located primarily, but not exclusively, within one hundred miles of Houston. I've included the results here because they provide a good indication of the best old roses for the Gulf South region. I wish I could offer this kind of survey information for every region of the South, but to my knowledge there haven't yet been any polls taken in other areas.

Most Fragrant Rose

1. 'Sombreuil'
2. 'Comte de Chambord' and 'Souvenir de la Malmaison'
3. 'Autumn Damask,' 'Felicia,' and 'Marquise Bocella'
4. 'Baronne Prevost,' 'Kazanlik,' 'Mrs. B. R. Cant,' 'Mme. Isaac Pereire,' "Maggie," and 'Paul Neyron'

Best Climbers

1. 'Mermaid'
2. 'Rêve d'Or' and 'Sombreuil'
3. 'Climbing Souvenir de la Malmaison'
4. 'Lady Banks' Rose'
5. 'Jaune Desprez,' "Maggie," 'Prosperity,' and 'Vanity'

Best for Landscape / Garden Color

1. 'Archduke Charles' and 'Cramoisi Supérieur'
2. 'Mutabilis' and 'Old Blush'
3. 'La Marne'
4. 'Cécile Brünner,' 'Clotilde Soupert,' 'Duchesse de Brabant,' 'The Fairy,' 'Lady Banks' Rose,' and "Maggie"

Best Flower (form / beauty)

1. 'Souvenir de la Malmaison'
2. 'Sombreuil'
3. 'Duchesse de Brabant'
4. 'Clotilde Soupert' and 'Comte de Chambord'
5. "Margaret Sharpe's Rose," 'Mme. Isaac Pereire,' 'Mrs. B. R. Cant,' and 'Paul Neyron'

Easiest to Propagate

1. 'Old Blush'
2. 'Clotilde Soupert' and 'Cramoisi Superieur'
3. 'The Fairy,' "Maggie," 'Marquise Bocella,' 'Prosperity,' and 'Mevrouw Nathalie Nypels'

Easiest to Grow

1. 'Mutabilis'
2. 'Old Blush'
3. 'Duchesse de Brabant'
4. 'Chestnut Rose,' 'Lady Banks' Rose,' and 'Prosperity'
5. 'Champneys' Pink Cluster,' 'Cramoisi Supérieur,' 'Green Rose,' 'Kronprinzessin Viktoria,' 'La Marne,' 'Mermaid,' 'Paul Neyron,' and 'Souvenir de la Malmaison'

Most Disease Resistant

1. 'Lady Banks' Rose'
2. 'Chestnut Rose,' 'Duchesse de Brabant,' 'Monsieur Tillier,' and 'Mrs. B. R. Cant'
3. 'Isabella Sprunt,' 'Mermaid,' 'Mrs. Dudley Cross,' 'Mutabilis,' "Natchitoches Noisette," 'Old Blush,' 'Russell's Cottage Rose,' 'Safrano,' and 'Swamp Rose'

The Houston Rose Society also conducted a survey of favorite roses and included a class for "Old Garden Rose Favorites." Following are their top five.

1. 'Souvenir de la Malmaison'
2. 'Mutabilis'
3. 'Sombreuil'
4. 'Mrs. B. R. Cant'
5. 'Kronprinzessin Viktoria' and 'Marquise Bocella'

Antique Roses by Class

THE roses chosen for this section are grouped according to class, and with each class is included a brief outline of its history, landscape uses, hardiness factors, flowering habits, and other information. Following these introductions to the various classes are more specific descriptions of each variety. Since some of our best roses have not been positively identified, you will find them listed under their study names with double quotation marks rather than with single ones, which are reserved for varieties that have been positively identified.

Generally, the classes and their varieties are presented in approximate chronological order of their date of introduction, to provide a sense of evolution within the sphere of old roses. Because the pronunciation of French names does not come naturally to most of us, I have included a syllable-by-syllable approximation. Near the end of the section of varietal and class descriptions is information on their culture and propagation.

Species and Related Hybrids

SPECIES roses may be defined as those growing in wild populations in nature. Most of the roses listed here are species, the remainder being hybrids that retain many species characteristics. All those included tend to be of excellent vigor and are for the most part disease resistant. They are good choices for naturalizing and will often grow well without attention if planted properly and given some care during the first year or so. Species roses are particularly valuable for use with native perennials and other wildflowers since both groups of plants tend to thrive with minimal attention.

Species roses can impart a natural elegance to the landscape and fit well into a wide variety of settings. Most bloom only in the spring and spend the rest of their energy producing healthy, abundant foliage. The spring display is well worth waiting for each year. Some species roses also produce handsome fruit (hips) that add to their attractiveness in the landscape and have value as wildlife food as well. Most tend to be fairly large and look their best when not cramped in the garden. Although many are climbers, with a minimum of training and pruning they can be grown as large shrubs.

'MUSK ROSE'

Rosa moschata
species   1540   6'–10'

English horticulturist, author, and artist Graham Thomas rediscovered the true 'Musk Rose' in 1963 and considered it one of the most exciting events of his rose-collecting career. Long associated with Shakespearian and other literature, the true 'Musk Rose'—which had been replaced in the nursery industry by a relative that bloomed only in spring and had different foliage—has only recently been made available once more.

We owe the later rediscovery in America of this fine rose to Carl Cato, Ruth Knopf, and Marie and John Butler, old rose experts from the Southeast who meticulously researched it after first finding it in Elmwood Cemetery in Charlotte, North Carolina, then later in Hollywood Cemetery in Richmond, Virginia. A more detailed account of the rediscovery of the 'Musk Rose' may be found in Thomas Christopher's *In Search of Lost Roses* (Summit Books, 1989).

Charles Walker, president of the Heritage Rose Foundation, has both the double and single forms of this plant at his garden in Raleigh, North Carolina. These are among the most fragrant roses I have ever known. The aroma is sometimes described as being like beeswax and honey. It is a remarkable fragrance, said to duplicate the secretions of the male musk deer, a scent which has been a basis for costly perfumes since ancient times. The long bloom season, wonderful fragrance, and ease of culture should once again make this a popular rose for locations that can absorb a fairly large specimen.

The 'Musk Rose' presumably originated in India or southern China and then spread west to southern Europe and northern Africa. It came to England via Spain in 1521 and was in America by 1800. This rose

'Musk Rose'

prospers only in warm, humid climates where it can become large and everblooming. Cream-colored, medium-sized flowers appear in large clusters throughout the growing season, but most abundantly in spring and fall. The sweet fragrance is free in the air and most noticeable in the evening hours. The 'Musk Rose' is a parent of both the Noisette and Hybrid Musk classes. Spent flowers tend to dry and hang on the plant, creating a somewhat untidy appearance at the end of a bloom cycle. However, the 'Musk Rose' is well worth having just for its fragrance.

'Swamp Rose'

'Swamp Rose'

'SWEETBRIER'

Rosa eglanteria
species   possible prior to 1551   8′–10′

Clusters of single pink flowers occur in spring and are followed by orange-red, edible hips. 'Sweetbrier' is useful as a large shrub or climber and is known for its apple-scented foliage. The fragrance is especially strong immediately following a warm rain.

'SWAMP ROSE'

Rosa palustris scandens
species   1726   6′–8′

The 'Swamp Rose' is native from Louisiana eastward to Florida, occurring along streams and in marshes. Its ability to tolerate wet, poorly drained locations is rare among roses and adds to the value of the plant. The form most often found in old gardens in the South is double or semi-double. 'Swamp Rose' blooms in mid to late spring. Its stems are almost thornless, and the plant has a neat, weeping appearance that makes it attractive even when not in bloom. This form was in the collection of Empress Josephine of France (1763–1814) and was painted by Redouté, famed Belgian flower portraitist, as *R. hudsoniana scandens*. Fragrance is excellent, and the soft pink flowers can nearly cover the gracefully arching limbs for several weeks each spring.

The 'Swamp Rose' has been highly disease and insect resistant in my garden. I enjoy a specimen near our front entrance but must prune it each year after the spring bloom because it is becoming quite large. When pruning, it's best to remove a few old canes and shape the plant rather than to give it an overall shearing. This approach will leave its beautiful natural structure intact. It is very adaptable in terms of soil and water conditions, thriving in both wet and dry locations. Iron chlorosis (yellowing of the foliage caused by an iron deficiency) can occur in very alkaline soils.

'CHEROKEE'

Rosa laevigata
species   1759   5'–15'

Georgians may be well aware of their state flower, but 'Cherokee' is little known elsewhere in the South. This disfavor derives from an unfortunate confusion of 'Cherokee' with the 'Macartney Rose' (*R. bracteata*), a distinct species that is a true pest to Southern stockmen and farmers. 'Cherokee' is a climber to fifteen feet or more, with neat, dark green leaves. In spring it blooms profusely, bearing flowers of five pure white petals that soon drop cleanly to disclose the star-shaped sepals. It makes a good hedge, climber, or pillar and is valuable for its ease of growth and disease resistance, although the stems are quite thorny.

'VIRGINIANA'

Rosa virginiana
species   before 1807   3'–6'

Bright pink single flowers adorn the neat, bushy shrub, making *R. virginiana* a valuable landscape plant. Colorful fall foliage and large, orange hips add to the seasonal interest of this spring-blooming plant. Native to the eastern U.S., it thrives in a wide variety of conditions, but prefers neutral or acid soils.

'CARNEA'

Rosa multiflora 'Carnea'
species hybrid 1804   15'–20'

This is an early forebear of many of the rambler roses. It reached England in 1804 via the East India Company and has clusters of small, very full double pink flowers. Like the 'Swamp Rose,' 'Carnea' was part of Empress Josephine's collection at Malmaison and was painted there by Redoute. Although it blooms only in

'Cherokee Rose'

'Carnea'

'Yellow Lady Banks' is an impressive climbing rose.

'White Lady Banks'

spring, it creates a memorable display, throwing waves of pink blossoms over buildings, banks, dead trees, or fences—any place it can ramble. Like many other hybrids of R. *multiflora*, 'Carnea' is susceptible to powdery mildew and should be planted where there is bright sun and good air circulation. When at its best, it delivers a splendid display with which few roses can compare.

'LADY BANKS' ROSE'

Rosa banksia 'Alba Plena'
species   1807   10'–20'

'Lady Banks' Rose,' commonly known as Banksia, is an outstanding climbing plant for the South. The date of introduction given here is the date the plant was discovered in China and imported to England. It was named for the wife of the Royal Horticultural Society's president. Although usually treated as a climber and provided with structural support, it does fine with no support at all. Grown this way, Banksias require a great deal of space and can easily reach fifteen feet in diameter and height. The only real enemy of this plant is severe cold.

During the disastrous winter of 1983–84, Banksias and some other tender roses were damaged as far

'Yellow Lady Banks'

'Prairie Rose'

south as central Texas. The flowers are double, about an inch in diameter, and last three to four weeks in early spring. The graceful arching habit of the thornless canes and its vigor and drought tolerance place this among the most useful of all old roses. The white form is rarer than the yellow one, which is commonly sold in garden centers over much of the South. The white form has a fairly strong fragrance, said to be reminiscent of violets.

Rosa banksia 'Lutea' is the yellow form which was introduced to England in 1824. Other than the stronger fragrance of the white form and the flower colors, the two plants are quite similar. Banksias are difficult to root by conventional methods. Commercial nurseries propagate them from semi-hardwood cuttings during the summer under an intermittent mist system. Once established, they often live to be very old and graceful plants. Banksias are among the most disease resistant and vigorous of all roses.

'PRAIRIE ROSE'

Rosa setigera
species   1810   4'–6'

The 'Prairie Rose' is native to Texas and the South. Arching branches, clusters of single, bright pink flowers that open in late spring, and the handsome red hips that follow them characterize this easily grown plant. A thornless form of *R. setigera* 'Serena' was given to me by Dr. Robert Basye, and I, in turn, have given it to several nurseries. The plant does not sucker, but branch tips will root readily when they touch the ground. The 'Prairie Rose' is very drought and cold tolerant and especially appropriate for low maintenance plantings.

'Chestnut Rose'

'CHESTNUT ROSE'

Rosa roxburghii
species   prior to 1814   5'–7'

The 'Chestnut Rose' is truly distinct. The double pink form was introduced from a Chinese garden to England in 1820 and sent to America soon afterwards. It has been found persevering despite neglect in a number of old Texas and Southern gardens. Flowers occur primarily in May and June and are followed by bristly hips that resemble chestnut cases and fall off while green. Flaking, light brown bark on older plants, and leaves composed of a great many leaflets (up to fifteen), make the 'Chestnut Rose' easily remembered. Although not particularly fragrant, the flowers are quite beautiful and occur over a long period. The plant is also very disease resistant. Houston area old rose rustlers first found this plant at the Ammon Underwood home in East Columbia in 1983. Few roses are as distinctive and useful as a specimen in the garden.

'SEVEN SISTERS'

Rosa multiflora 'Platyphylla'
Hybrid Multiflora   1817   15'–20'

Like many of the other roses described in this book, 'Seven Sisters' thrives only in the South where winters are relatively mild. There is much confusion concerning the identity of this rose, but the real 'Seven Sisters' is an impressive, once-blooming rambler with large clusters of small flowers in shades of pink, mauve, purple, and cream that change as the flowers age. 'Seven Sisters' is a legendary rose in the South. Like most of its Multiflora kin, it is susceptible to powdery mildew and should be planted in a sunny, open area or treated to prevent or control the disease. Its display lasts for several weeks each spring and is worth the wait to see.

'RUSSELL'S COTTAGE ROSE'

R. multiflora 'Russelliana'
Hybrid Multiflora   prior to 1837   5'–7'

This rose is occasionally found at old sites in Texas and the Gulf South. Although a spring-only bloomer, it is very tough and disease resistant. The medium-sized, double flowers occur in mid-spring and are a rich purple, changing to lilac as they age. The fragrance is intense and Damask-like. It is a useful plant for the background or as a specimen. The hips are orange and large. An interesting foliage characteristic of this rose is the pine-like scent of new leaves.

My 'Russell's Cottage Rose' was a gift from native plant expert Lynn Lowrey. It was identified for me by Joyce Demitts of Heritage Roses in California. While visiting the Huntington Botanical Garden I described my "mystery rose" to Joyce and she asked whether I had noticed the pine scent of the new foliage. When I said that I had, she took me to a labeled specimen in full bloom and said, "I think this is your rose!" It's exciting to identify a rose you have been growing and wondering about for several years.

'Russell's Cottage Rose'

'Fortune's Double Yellow'

'WHITE CAROLINA RAMBLER'

Rosa anemoneflora
species   1844   10′–15′

This hybrid species was found by the great plant hunter Robert Fortune in China. When it was shipped back to England, it was generally panned by everyone who saw it. Then someone had the bright idea that *R. anemoneflora* might be sulking in the cool, wet English climate and sent it to the American South where, like its Banksia cousins, it responded wonderfully. Somewhat like white 'Lady Banks' Rose,' it is covered in the spring with one-inch white flowers; the outer petals are smooth, but the centers are tufted and shaggy. It has a violet-like fragrance and an early spring bloom time like that of the Banksias.

'FORTUNE'S DOUBLE YELLOW'

Rosa x odorata pseudindica
miscellaneous old garden rose   1845   6′–10′

This rose bears the name of its finder, Robert Fortune, a young Scottish undergardener who discovered it in the newly opened China of 1845. Other names for this rose are "Beauty of Glazenwood" and "Gold of Ophir." Fortune's personal account of the event is as follows: "On entering one of the (mandarin's) gardens on a fine morning in May, I was struck with a mass of yellow flowers which completely covered a distant part of the wall. . . . To my surprise and delight I found that I had discovered a most beautiful new yellow climbing rose" ("A Letter from Robert Fortune," *Journal of the Royal Horticultural Society*, Volume 6).

Actually, the color is more buff-apricot with rose-colored rim on the outer edges of the petals. Slender, apple-jade foliage lends a delicate appearance. Gertrude Jekyll praised it as being "indispensable on account of its grace and beauty." 'Fortune's Double Yellow' blooms for several weeks in spring, and, like many of the other old roses, it flowers more prolifically after several years' growth. It is moderately disease resistant and fairly thorny.

'FORTUNIANA'

Rosa x fortuniana
miscellaneous old garden rose   1850   8′–10′

This rose is another of Robert Fortune's discoveries. Its advantages include the ability to thrive in poor, dry, sandy soils and its disease resistance, making it popular as an understock in Australia and parts of Florida. 'Fortuniana' is closely related to the Banksias, having the same cascading habit and similar leaflets, but its blooms are larger and only white. Some experts speculate that it is a cross between *R. laevigata* ('Cherokee') and *R. banksia* 'Alba Plena,' (white 'Lady Banks' Rose'),

'Anemone Rose'

'Fortuniana'

'Vielchenblau'

and characteristics of both species are apparent when the plant is examined closely. It has sometimes been sold erroneously as white Banksia. Fragrance is good, but the real value is in the ease of culture and graceful effect from this plant, which blooms about the same times as the Banksias each spring.

'ANEMONE ROSE'

Hybrid Laevigata   1896   6′–10′

"Pink Cherokee" is another name for this unusual rose that is a cross between the 'Cherokee' and a Tea. Somewhat like a clematis in appearance, with large, pink flowers touched with a rose blush, it blooms very early in the spring and grows rapidly but does not rebloom. Because of the tender types in its family tree, it is not dependably cold hardy beyond the deep South. Foliage is healthy, as are the ferocious thorns that arm the stems.

'VIELCHENBLAU'

R. *multiflora* 'Vielchenblau'
Hybrid Multiflora   1909   10′–15′

This highly fragrant rambler created quite a sensation when it was introduced as "The Blue Rose." Actually the blossoms are purple or crimson with streaks of white, and they fade to a grayish-blue. Bright gold stamens appear very prominent against the dark, dull color of the flowers. When planted against a light background or with white or pale roses, this rose is spectacular. 'Vielchenblau' is nearly thornless and is more disease resistant than most Hybrid Multifloras.

'Mermaid' is a popular wall rose.

'Mermaid'

'MERMAID'

Hybrid Bracteata   1918   10′–20′

'Mermaid' is reported to be a cross between *R. bracteata* ('Macartney Rose') and an old yellow Tea Rose. It is very vigorous and thorny, but also beautiful and fragrant. Sprinkled among the shiny, healthy foliage, the flowers bloom from late spring until frost. They are large, single, and sulfur-yellow in color, with petals that shed cleanly. 'Mermaid' is very popular in England, where it is used extensively as a wall rose in the gardens of Hampton Court, Hever Castle, and numerous other estates. Jack Harkness, a past president of the Royal National Rose Society, gives 'Mermaid' his five-star rating and lists it among the ten finest roses of all time. It thrives in Texas and the South and is only occasionally damaged by cold in those areas. 'Mermaid' is a wonderful rose where it can be allowed to grow freely, but its thorns are truly awesome, so placing it where it can grab people with them is not recommended!

asye's
urple
ose'

'Basye's Purple Rose'

Rosa foliolosa x R. rugosa
shrub   1968   5'–6'

'Basye's Purple Rose' is a cross between *R. foliolosa* (native to Arkansas) and *R. rugosa* (native to Japan). It was bred by Dr. Robert Basye, a retired university professor and active rose breeder from Caldwell, Texas, in his search for hardy, drought tolerant, disease resistant cultivars. 'Basye's Purple Rose' met all these criteria, but he rejected it as a "jewel in the rough." The ravishingly fragrant, large, single flowers appear in profusion during the spring on a large, healthy shrub. Dr. Basye considers this rose to be a truly unusual color: royal purple with prominent gold stamens. When grown on its own roots it does sucker and can spread rather rapidly. It was given to me by Dr. Basye in 1983. I gave stock material to the Antique Rose Emporium at Brenham, Texas, where it has been propagated and distributed. Like most roses having *R. rugosa* parentage, it prefers a neutral to slightly acid soil.

'Memorial Rose'

R. wichuraiana
late 1800s in Europe   2'–3' × 20'

R. wichuraiana is a native of Japan and Korea that was brought to Europe in the late 1800s. Its neat, glossy foliage and cold hardiness have made it popular in breeding modern roses such as 'New Dawn' and 'Silver Moon.'

I received a very useful form of *R. wichuraiana* from Dr. Robert Basye in 1985. Dr. Basye received it from the Princeton Nursery in New Jersey, where it appeared as a chance seedling in about 1965. It is a nearly thornless selection with shining foliage that is almost evergreen in the South. Single white flowers appear in clusters during late spring and summer and ripen to small bright red hips in fall. Best use is as a groundcover where individual plants may spread twenty feet, forming mounds one to three feet tall. Insect and disease resistance are good, but a neutral to acid soil is preferred; alkaline soils may result in severe yellowing of the foliage and lack of vigor due to iron chlorosis.

Another useful form is *R. wichuraiana* 'Poteriifolia,' which I received from Dr. Skip March at the National Arboretum in 1984. The original plants were collected from natural stands along the coast at Murotozaki, Kochi Prefecture, Japan. It is less vigorous than *R. wichuraiana* but also useful as a ground cover where its small, pure white single flowers appear periodically throughout the growing season. Individual plants typically spread six to eight feet and may reach two to three feet in height. Foliage is shiny, dark green and branches are prickly. Plants of both these species were given to the Antique Rose Emporium, where they are currently available.

'Old Blush'

Chinas

A THOUSAND YEARS before the birth of Christ, the Chinese had bred their single-flowering native roses into true garden types. The revolutionary characteristic of these roses was that they were everblooming. The everblooming quality of all modern roses can be traced back to these early Chinas.

Individual blossoms of most Chinas are not spectacular. These roses are not likely to win "Best of Show," but their profusion of flowers, their disease resistance, and their typically long, healthy life more than compensate. It is not unusual to find specimens of China Roses a hundred years old or older surviving entirely without human care in Texas and the South. Bloom is heaviest in mid-spring, with sprinklings of flowers all summer. Another heavy bloom in fall usually follows the first good rains in September or October.

Chinas are useful as hedges, specimen plants, or borders. If pruned severely, most of them can be easily maintained as small, rounded plants. They respond well to heavy pruning in winter but seem to resent it in summer. When allowed to grow with only dead or weak wood removed, they slowly attain large size.

Dean S. Reynolds Hole, the English rosarian and cleric who is credited with the formation of the Royal National Rose Society, summed up his praise for the China Roses in his book *Our Gardens* published in 1899. "There is no other claimant to the title of *Semper florens*, bestowed by an ecumenical council of botanists upon the China or monthly roses—'*Semper, ubique, ab omnibus*'—always, everywhere, for all."

In addition to describing here some of the best varieties of China Roses for the South, I have included a few roses that rose rustlers have found but have not yet been able to identify positively. Perhaps you can compare these to roses in your area and help provide information concerning their identities.

'Old Blush'

1752   5'–6'

Other names for this rose are "Parson's Pink China," "Old Pink Daily," "Common Monthly," and "Daisy Rose." This thrifty rose is one of the most common— yet pleasant—of the old roses. It bears medium, semi-double, light pink blossoms in many-flowered clusters, which often blush a dark rose on the outer edge of the petals in strong sun. 'Old Blush' is constantly in flower, with a really heavy flush in the spring. The bush is up-right in habit and may bloom eleven months of the year in the Gulf South. When at its peak in spring, 'Old Blush' can rival an azalea in full bloom. Flower quality becomes poor during the heat of summer but improves radically with the first cool days of fall.

'Cramoisi Supérieur'

(krah mwah *zee* soo pay ry *uhr*)
1832   4'–6'

Another commonly used name for this rose is "Agrippina." It is said to resemble closely the original red China, *R. chinensis* 'Semperflorens.' 'Cramoisi Supérieur' has velvety, rich crimson flowers with a silvery reverse in a double, cupped form and, like all Chinas, is very nearly everblooming in this climate. The leaves are small, dark green, and very healthy. 'Cramoisi Supérieur' is excellent for hedges, at the back of the flower border, as a shrub, or as a pot rose. One of Gertrude Jekyll's favorites, it is a valuable and beautiful land-scape plant that provides almost continuous color.

'Old Blush' adds old-fashioned charm.

'Cramoisi Supérieur' in an old San Antonio garden

'Cramoisi Supérieur' resembles the original red China rose.

'Archduke Charles' is a more refined rose than most Chinas.

'Archduke Charles' is part of a lovely cottage garden filled with tall bearded iris and shasta daisies.

'Louis Philippe'

(loo-*wee* fee-*leep*)
1834   3′–5′

One of the first Texas plantings of 'Louis Philippe' was at the Lynchburg home of Lorenzo de Zavala, Texas's minister to France in 1834, who brought this and other roses back with him from the Court of St. Cloud. His homesite and cemetery are now swallowed by industrial development along the Houston ship channel. The double, cupped flowers of 'Louis Philippe' are dark crimson with blush edges on the center petals. Constant flowering occurs from early spring until winter—and an occasional bloom may occur during winter warm spells. 'Louis Philippe' and other red Chinas are commonly confused, and even experts are uncertain about their positive identity. Natives of the deep South usually refer to any red China rose as 'Louis Philippe.'

'Archduke Charles'

prior to 1837   3′–5′

The best description of 'Archduke Charles' comes from the premier American old rosarian, Ethelyn Emery Keays, who said in *Old Roses:* "The full, lasting flower with outer petals of deep rose-red opens in a cupped shape, enclosing in the cup smaller petals of whitish pink to real white. . . . The rose color gradually creeps in and over the pale center so entirely that the flower becomes a rose colored bloom." She adds: "A fine old rose, much admired in the past" (Earl M. Coleman Publishing, 1935, 1978). 'Archduke Charles' has a more refined flower than most Chinas. A single bush may appear to bear blooms of several different colors simultaneously because the flowers' colors change rapidly as they age.

'HERMOSA'

1840   3'–4'

The famous Southern nurseryman Thomas Affleck of Natchez, Mississippi, and Gay Hill, Texas, said of 'Hermosa' in 1856, "Still one of the best!" A gracious blue-green bushy plant of moderate growth, 'Hermosa' bears full, medium-sized flowers in clusters of a subtle, old-rose shade and is nearly always in bloom. Good for mass plantings and useful as a pot rose, 'Hermosa' is sometimes classified as a Bourbon.

'THE GREEN ROSE'

Rosa chinensis 'Viridiflora'
prior to 1845   3'–4'

Rosarians may argue whether or not this flower is beautiful, but all agree 'The Green Rose' is truly different. British rose authority Jack Harkness describes it as an "engaging monstrosity." Flower arrangers find the bronzy green flowers useful and long-lasting subjects. They have a spicy scent and become bronzy-colored in the fall. 'The Green Rose' is found in many old gardens of the South and is easily grown.

'MUTABILIS'

Rosa chinensis 'Mutabilis'
prior to 1896   4'–7'

This most interesting rose is of unknown origin and grows to about six feet with very bronzy young growth. The single flowers open buff-yellow, changing to pink and finally crimson; often flowers of all three colors appear simultaneously. It is sometimes called the "Butterfly Rose" because its blooms resemble those graceful insects. 'Mutabilis' is a useful but twiggy shrub that is recommended as a wall plant by some experts. The

'Hermosa'

'Green Rose'

'Mutabilis'

'Ducher'

plant is normally grown as a medium-sized shrub, but a magnificent specimen at Kiftsgate Court, Gloucestershire, England, is described in Gault and Synge's *Dictionary of Roses in Colour* (Michael Joseph, 1971) as covering a wall twenty feet in height and as wide. Although occasionally bothered by powdery mildew during the spring, 'Mutabilis' can be a fine addition to the Southern garden. I have never found a really old specimen of 'Mutabilis' growing in a Southern garden, but a number have been planted in recent years. A beautiful specimen adorns the split rail fence in front of the University of Texas Cultural Center at Winedale. It is at least seven feet tall with an equal spread, and is almost constantly in flower.

'COMTESSE DU CAYLA'

1920   3'–5'

Named for the beautiful mistress of Louis XVIII, 'Comtesse du Cayla' has handsome, coppery-pink flowers with coppery foliage to match. Like most Chinas, it is almost constantly in bloom with semi-double flowers and is a good garden subject. Fragrance is better than in most Chinas.

'DUCHER'

1869   3'–4'

This is the only white China rose I know, and for that reason it is valuable as a garden plant. The flower is rather full and more refined than that of most Chinas, except perhaps 'Archduke Charles.' The flowers are fragrant, creamy white, profuse, and frequent. The foliage is a dark, rich green and provides a handsome setting for the flowers.

"MARTHA GONZALES"

a found rose   2′–3′

Pamela Puryear, historian and rosarian from Navasota, Texas, found this beautiful rose growing as a hedge in the Navasota garden of Martha Gonzales. It has been given to the Antique Rose Emporium and San Antonio area nurseries for possible introduction. There is some evidence that the true identity of "Martha Gonzales" is 'Fabvier,' an old, single or semi-double red China. "Martha Gonzales" is a very compact growing plant ideal for low hedges (18–24 inches high). It is disease resistant and almost constantly in flower with two-inch bright red blooms. The petals fall cleanly from the flower heads, but since "Martha Gonzales" flowers so freely, the bloom stems and heads are best removed periodically with hedge shears to promote more frequent displays.

"HIGHWAY 290 PINK BUTTONS"

a found rose   1′–2′

This fascinating little rose has been found growing in old cemeteries and gardens throughout south and central Texas. It appears to be a relative of *Rosa chinensis* 'Minima.' Flowers are double and about the size of a nickel, and the plant is a dense growing one ideal for a low hedge or pot specimen. It has a habit of aborting buds before they open if there is any kind of environmental stress such as drought or intense heat. I have had experienced gardeners tell me that they have had this plant in their families for at least a hundred years.

"OLD GAY HILL RED CHINA"

a found rose   4′–6′

Tommy Adams and I found this rose on an old homesite near where Thomas Affleck had his famous nursery

"Martha Gonzales"

in the 1850s. It is much like "Martha Gonzales" but larger growing and more vigorous. Dark green foliage provides a nice background for the intensely red semi-double flowers.

"PAM'S PINK"

a found rose   3′–5′

This rose was found by Pamela Puryear in an old Navasota, Texas, garden. It is more refined than most Chinas, having rich, pink buds with darker pink inner petals showing darker veining.

Noisettes

THE Noisettes, a group of graceful, everblooming shrubs and climbers, were the first class of roses to originate in the United States. Early Noisettes have clusters of small flowers, while the later ones have larger blossoms with fewer per cluster. These later varieties resulted from crosses with roses from the Tea class.

John Champneys, a rice planter from Charleston, South Carolina, raised the first Noisette by crossing the Musk Rose known in Shakespeare's day with 'Old Blush.' He named it 'Champneys' Pink Cluster.' A few years later, Philippe Noisette, a florist from Charleston and a friend of Champneys's, raised a seedling from Champneys's rose. In 1817, Noisette sent his rose to his brother Louis in Paris, who named it 'Blush Noisette.' (It appears that the rose currently being sold under that name by the nursery trade both here and abroad is not the authentic 'Blush Noisette.') The French eagerly received and expanded the new rose class because of its heavy clustering bloom, musky scent, and strong, healthy growth. Although considered more susceptible to cold than most classes, the Noisettes were immensely popular and are well adapted to the Southern states. Their Musk Rose ancestry insures a good floral display in the fall as well as in the spring. As a rule, however, they are not as resistant to black spot and mildew as are the Teas and Chinas.

Many of the Noisettes have the ability to create a landscape effect unique among roses. Whether grown on walls, fences, arbors, or even trees, the climbing varieties are indispensable to a garden in which a period effect is desired.

'CHAMPNEYS' PINK CLUSTER'

circa 1811   4′–8′

This is a very fragrant rose that bears 1 1/2-inch to 2-inch double, pink flowers in large clusters throughout the season. It is effective when used against a fence or wall, or as a single specimen, where it becomes a rather large, upright shrub. It is a vigorous plant but is susceptible to black spot.

'Champneys' Pink Cluster'

'AIMÉE VIBERT'

1828 6'–10'

A vigorous climber or larger shrub, 'Aimée Vibert' has enjoyed wide popularity in England and France. Dull green foliage is a foil for the well scented, small clusters of pale pink flowers. 'Aimée Vibert' was a favorite of Gertrude Jekyll and appears in several photographs in her book *Roses for English Gardens* (Baron Publishing Co.). It has been confused in the trade with the Hybrid Musk 'Prosperity,' which is commonly found in Southern gardens. 'Prosperity' has larger flower clusters and shiny dark green foliage.

'LAMARQUE'

1830 8'–10'

A fine climber, 'Lamarque' is the result of a cross between 'Blush Noisette' and 'Parks' Yellow Tea-Scented China.' The double flowers are moderate in size and white with yellow centers. Blooms occur in clusters, and fragrance is excellent. A specimen of 'Lamarque' found by Extension Horticulturist Greg Grant in San Antonio has been verified to date back to 1890. Several very large and handsome specimens may be found tumbling over garden walls along Church Street in the restored area of Charleston, South Carolina. The foliage of 'Lamarque' is unusually dark green and healthy. It is one of the finest climbing roses for year-round garden effect.

'Lamarque'

'Lamarque' is a dramatic Noisette climber.

'JAUNE DESPREZ'

(zhohn day *pray*)
1830   15'–20'

The medium-yellow, quartered blooms of 'Jaune Desprez' are shaded with apricot and have green centers. They are wonderfully fragrant and were much admired in Charleston, South Carolina, during the 1840s. This rose is another distinctive climber that can create a beautiful garden picture, blooming heavily in spring and fall with scattered flowers throughout the summer. It is ideal for pergolas.

'Jaune Desprez'

'CHROMATELLA'

1843   12'–20'

'Chromatella,' most famous for being an alleged parent of the revered 'Maréchal Niel,' is in turn descended from 'Lamarque,' and has large double, pale yellow blooms with golden-yellow centers. The partially open flowers are bell shaped and very similar to those of 'Maréchal Niel.' Fragrance is excellent, but, like its more famous offspring, 'Chromatella' is sometimes challenging to get established.

'JEANNE D'ARC'

(zhahn dark)
1848   5'–8'

The flowers of this rose are small and pure white. They appear in large clusters and, like those of most other Noisettes, are outstandingly fragrant. If the faded blooms are allowed to stay on the plant and mature, they ripen into large clusters of handsome red fruit. Sometimes in late fall, both flower and fruit appear together and make an impressive combination. This rose is sometimes classed as a Polyantha.

'Jeanne d'Arc'

'CÉLINE FORESTIER'

(say lean fohr res tee ay)
1858   10'–15'

Strong, spicy scent accompanies the lovely flowers of 'Céline Forestier,' which are quartered, flat, and creamy yellow. The pastel coloring is enhanced by the green eye at the flower's center. It is sometimes slow to establish, but mature plants can be spectacular.

'Céline Forestier' has creamy yellow blooms.

'Maréchal Niel'

'MARÉCHAL NIEL'

(mah ray *shal* neel)
1864   10′–15′

This magnificent rose was legendary during the nineteenth century and early in the twentieth. The full, quartered, buttery yellow blossoms have a unique and memorable fragrance. 'Maréchal Niel' is very sensitive to cold and difficult to establish. It appears to have degenerated over the years or perhaps acquired a virus that has weakened the plant. Until a vigorous source for propagation material can be assured, 'Maréchal Niel' will probably have to remain only in the memory of those of us who have seen and experienced its beauty and fragrance. Considered by many to be the finest yellow rose ever created, it is a moderate climber that blooms prolifically all season.

An apparently vigorous specimen of 'Maréchal 'Niel,' verified to be more than fifty years old, has recently been located in a central Texas garden. Budwood and cuttings are currently being evaluated in several locations throughout the South to see if it retains its legendary vigor. Approximately one year after plants have been distributed, they do appear more vigorous. Trials are also being done with various understocks to see if this beautiful rose can once again be propagated and made available.

'Rêve d'Or'

'RÊVE D'OR'

(rehv dohr)
1869 10′–12′

'Rêve d'Or' is a useful wall rose and climber with beige-yellow, globular flowers. Flower color is more peachy in spring, and flowers appear in clusters of three to five on many laterals. Later in the season clusters are smaller with one to three blooms hanging down from the ends of new branches. Although the plant is often listed as being nearly thornless, those grown by myself and others do not bear this out. 'Rêve d'Or' is a beautiful rose, but it does not rebloom as well as the other Noisettes in my garden. It is very disease resistant and blooms early in the season.

'WILLIAM ALLEN RICHARDSON'

1878 10′–15′

'William Allen Richardson' is a sport of 'Rêve d'Or' and is known for its vigor and ability to be in almost continuous flower. Foliage is dark green with a copper tint and flowers are double and buff with orange-apricot centers. 'William Allen Richardson' is considered by English rose expert Peter Beales to be the last important Noisette introduction.

'Mme. Alfred Carrière' espaliered against a wall at Sissinghurst's White Garden

'MME. ALFRED CARRIÈRE'

(kah ree *ehr*)
1879 15′–20′

The buds on this vigorous plant are large and similar to typical Hybrid Teas. The two-inch flowers open pale lavender-pink but quickly fade to pure white. Fragrance is outstanding, but this rose is fairly susceptible to black spot and mildew. 'Mme. Alfred Carrière' is famous in England for the displays it creates on walls.

'NASTARANA'

1879   3'–4'

Large clusters of medium-sized, pure white, fragrant flowers are produced almost constantly on this upright, three- to four-foot plant. 'Nastarana' is reported to have originated in Iran from a cross between *R. moschata* and *R. chinensis*; it was popular in old Persian rose gardens. The fruit is red-orange when ripe and occurs in large clusters. Although susceptible to mildew and black spot, 'Nastarana' is a tough and attractive rose that blooms continuously and prolifically.

'CLAIRE JACQUIER'

(zhock *yehr*)
1888   15'–20'

This is a vigorous climber with clusters of yolk-yellow buds that open to blowsy, double, cream-colored blooms. The flowers are shapely and of medium size. They have good fragrance and rebloom in the summer and fall.

'MARY WASHINGTON'

1891   6'–8'

'Mary Washington' is like some of the early, small-flowered Noisettes with its semi-double, pale pink flowers on a neat attractive plant. It may be used as a small climber or shrub. 'Mary Washington' has outstanding fragrance and is one of the most profuse bloomers to be found.

"NATCHITOCHES NOISETTE"

(*nak* uh *tish*)
a found rose   4'–6'

There seems to be some question as to whether this rose is really a Noisette, but it seems to fit better here than anywhere else. I found this rose marking a gravesite in the old cemetery in Natchitoches, Louisiana. The rather small (1 1/2-inch), semi-double flowers are light pink and China-like with darker pink reverses on the petals. They bloom in medium-sized clusters and have a light Noisette fragrance. The plant from which I took cuttings was in bloom at Christmas and tends to be in flower much of the year. Hodges Gardens near Many, Louisiana, has a rooted cutting from the original, planted among the China Roses. "Natchitoches Noisette" is a little like 'Champneys' Pink Cluster' but with much better disease resistance and a somewhat less intense fragrance. It roots easily and responds well to pruning.

"Natchitoches Noisette"

Old European Roses

INCLUDED in this section are roses from a variety of classes that are worthy of consideration for landscapes in the South. Since they were developed primarily for shorter growing seasons and colder winters, they sometimes lack the vigor and disease resistance of roses from areas more like our own. However, they are significant historically for their long association with major events of Western history. Moreover, their beauty and fragrance have inspired great art and literature. The roses I have included in this section are arranged approximately in order of their introduction.

'THE APOTHECARY ROSE'

R. gallica officinalis
of great antiquity   3′–4′

Other names for this famous rose include 'Red Rose of Lancaster,' 'Rose of Provins,' and 'Double French Rose.' The scent-retaining qualities of this rose made it popular with apothecaries during the Middle Ages. Foliage is dark and grayish-green on erect, bushy plants. The flowers are quite large, semi-double, and of a beautiful light crimson color. Fragrant oval hips ripen in late summer and fall, adding color and interest to the garden. Various forms of *R. gallica* are often found in old cemeteries in the South—a testament to their durability. The Gallicas have had considerable influence on the more modern roses. Although susceptible to mildew, they are drought tolerant and insect resistant.

'The Apothecary Rose'

'ROSA MUNDI'

R. gallica versicolor
prior to 1581   3′–4′

This is the oldest striped rose on record and a sport of 'The Apothecary Rose' or 'Red Rose of Lancaster.' Named for "Fair Rosamund," mistress of King Henry

'Rosa Mundi'

II of England, it is a once-bloomer for a fairly long season in the spring, and it's useful as a low-growing rose in front of taller roses or other plants. The semi-double blooms are a striking combination of red stripes over a pink background, with yellow stamens in the center. Fragrance is modest, but landscape effect can be outstanding. There is a beautiful specimen in Rachel's Garden at The Hermitage near Nashville, Tennessee. A lovely mass of 'Rosa Mundi' is also included in the Pleasure Garden at Mt. Vernon.

'CELSIANA'

old European rose
prior to 1750   3'–5'

The parentage of this rose is unknown, but its scent is unmistakably Damask. Foliage is a light gray-green and form is compact. Semi-double flowers are large and borne in nodding clusters in spring, and they prominently display their yellow anthers. They are bright pink upon opening and fade after exposure to the sun.

'AUTUMN DAMASK'

old European rose
prior to 1819   4'–6'

Until the importation of China Roses, 'Autumn Damask' was the only rose in Europe that flowered again after the spring season. Flowers are double, light pink, and profusely fragrant with a Damask scent that is among the finest known. After its spring display, 'Autumn Damask' repeats modestly during the summer and fall. It is highly important as a parent to the Bourbon and Hybrid Perpetual classes of roses but also worthy of garden use. The shrub is compact and attractive.

'Autumn Damask'

'HIPPOLYTE'

a Gallica Rose of unknown parentage   4'–5'

Gallica Roses may still be found marking old cemetery plots and homesites throughout the South. They are very tough roses that tend to sucker and make small colonies in poor soils and form larger clumps under better growing conditions. 'Hippolyte' was found and collected by Joe Woodard, editor and publisher of *The Yellow Rose*, the newsletter of the Dallas Area Historical Rose Group. British rosarian Peter Beales describes it as "one of the nicest of the Gallicas." The flowers are beautifully formed and double, in shades of magenta-purple, clustering on thin, almost thornless stems that bow with their weight. Foliage is dark green and attractive. Gallicas are often susceptible to powdery mildew attacks in spring, but usually overcome the problem later in the season. Some gardeners consider their suckering habit a nuisance, but it can be an easy way to propagate and share good varieties that are otherwise hard to root. Gallicas may be grafted onto nonsuckering rootstocks, if preferred.

'Banshee' blooms on the left side of the path in Rachel's Garden at the Hermitage in Nashville.

'MADAME PLANTIER'

probably an Alba/Moschata cross
1835   4′–6′

Pale cream flowers change to pure white as their many petals unfold to form almost flat puffs revealing a green eye. Both foliage and stems are light gray-green, typical of the Alba class. Alba Roses are not well adapted to areas close to the Gulf but perform fairly well further north. This rose may be used as a lax shrub or a climber. It blooms only in spring and is a very fragrant addition to the garden.

'BANSHEE'

date of introduction and origin unknown
4′–5′

This rose has fascinated me for a number of years. It is said to be extremely cold hardy, yet it thrives in the hot, dry Texas summers. I obtained my first plant from Mrs. Mattie Rosprim, a talented College Station gardener, who first obtained it from her mother in the 1920s. I have observed what appears to be 'Banshee' in great profusion in Rachel's Garden at The Hermitage in Tennessee. Flowers are about 2 1/2 inches across,

'Salet' is one of the few Moss Roses that reblooms during summer and fall in the South.

double, and a pale pink that deepens near the centers. Stamens and petals are mixed together in a muddled but pleasing manner. In his book *Old Garden Roses*, Edward A. Bunyard describes the scent in this way: "It is remarkable for the penetrating Eau de Cologne scent, and will delight all lovers of scented Roses, being *sui generis* in this" (Earl M. Coleman Publishing, 1978). Stems are nearly thornless and disease resistance is excellent.

'Salet'

a Moss Rose
1854   3′–4′

The Moss Roses are well known for mossy glands on their calyxes and stems that secrete a resinous odor, causing the cut bloom to perfume the hand that holds it. The mossy sepals enclose beautifully formed, clear pink buds and open flowers that have many closely packed petals. 'Salet' reblooms as well as a modern Hybrid Tea does but is better adapted inland from the Gulf Coast at least a hundred or more miles.

'Deuil de Paul Fontaine'

a Moss Rose of unknown parentage
1873   3′–4′

The color of this rose is a very deep red to almost blackish-purple. The plant is compact and thorny. It is reported to rebloom well in the South.

'Mme. Louis Leveque'

a Moss Rose of unknown parentage
1898   3′–4′

The large flowers of 'Mme. Louis Leveque' are a soft, warm pink. The texture of the petals is like fine silk, and the flowers elegantly adorn their mossy nests. Foliage is dark green and stems are erect. 'Mme. Louis Leveque' is reported to rebloom in the South.

Teas

TEA Roses are exceptionally well suited to Southern climates and are often found as large bushes marking old homesites where they have cheerfully survived with no care whatsoever for decades. They are large and memorable roses, the kind people speak of with nostalgia. Tea Roses inherited their fragrance and large blossoms from the wild Tea Rose, *Rosa gigantea*, a native of the eastern Himalayan foothills. Their everblooming character is from *R. chinensis*, their other parent.

Many old Tea Roses resemble in form the typical high-centered Hybrid Teas of today, and are thus appreciated as cut flowers as well as garden plants. This class was very popular from the 1830s until its own more cold hardy descendants, the Hybrid Teas, superseded it at the turn of the century. As a rule, Teas have an upright habit, forming tall and sometimes narrow bushes with bronzy-red new foliage. In the Southern states, they bloom profusely in the spring and fall, with scattered summer flowers. Blossoms are spectacular and large in pastel pinks and yellows, with some reds and a few whites. Fragrance is distinctive, cool, and somewhat like that of dried tea leaves.

Most Teas have good resistance to black spot and seem to thrive in the heat of the South, although they are occasionally damaged by cold in northerly areas of our region. Tea Roses bloom until very cold weather. Accounts of early Texans gathering bouquets for Christmas and other midwinter events indicate that Tea Roses were considered an essential part of the garden at that time. The flower stems are weak and often bow gracefully with the weight of the large flowers. This was considered an elegant trait during Victorian times and is still appreciated by those who enjoy the many distinctive and easily grown roses that comprise the Tea class.

'Bon Silène'

'BON SILÈNE'

(*bohn* see *lehn*)
prior to 1837   4′–6′

'Bon Silène' is an old favorite that bears blossoms of a color unusual in a Tea Rose. The deep rose-colored buds are profuse and well scented. The shrub is often as broad as it is tall, and the foliage is usually healthy. This is one of the oldest Teas and still among the best.

'DEVONIENSIS'

1838   8'–10'

'Devoniensis' is somewhat like a climbing form of the famous 'Souvenir de la Malmaison.' It is an extremely beautiful rose sometimes known as the "Magnolia Rose." Flowers are creamy white, occasionally blushed with pink, double, and quite large.

'SAFRANO'

1839   5'–7'

A large specimen of 'Safrano' in the beautifully restored kitchen garden of the Mordecai House in Raleigh, North Carolina, fits in beautifully with the herbs and perennials. Bright apricot buds open to large, semi-double flowers of fawn or buff-tinted saffron. Mature plants assume an attractive mounded form, often as wide as they are tall. Foliage is disease resistant and handsome.

'SOMBREUIL'

(sohm *bruh* ee)
1850   6'–10'

The very strong Tea fragrance, shiny, dark green foliage, and spectacular creamy white flowers make this one of the most beautiful and useful of all roses. 'Sombreuil' is a rather mannerly climber, sometimes reaching eight to ten feet. The flowers are double and formal, almost like an 'Alba Plena' camellia, and often blushed with pink. Stems are very thorny, but the foliage is beautiful and unusually disease resistant. Heavy spring bloom with some summer flowers and a good profusion in the fall is typical for well established plants. 'Sombreuil' was a popular subject for glass houses in England where the winters are sometimes too severe for Tea Roses. A good flower specimen of this rose is spectacular.

'Safrano'

'Sombreuil' is a mannerly climber.

'GLOIRE DE DIJON'

(glwahr duh dee *zhohn*)
1853   10'–15'

This is a magnificent rose with flat, quartered, peachy pink blooms tinged apricot in the centers. A favorite among the clergy in England, 'Gloire de Dijon' has graced the south walls of homes and churches for over a century. It is excellent as a pillar or on a fence or trellis, but it's not as resistant to black spot as some of the other Teas.

'ISABELLA SPRUNT'

1855   4'–6'

'Isabella Sprunt' is a sport of 'Safrano' and similar in every way except in color. The dark, plum-colored foliage is a good foil for the pale yellow flowers. Like its parent, 'Isabella Sprunt' usually has attractive, healthy foliage.

'DUCHESSE DE BRABANT'

1857   3'–5'

Tulip-shaped, pink-rose flowers of medium size occur all season on a bush that is fairly small for a Tea Rose. Fragrance is excellent, although powdery mildew does find the foliage and buds irrestible, especially in spring. 'Duchesse de Brabant' was a favorite rose of Teddy Roosevelt, who wore a bud or flower frequently as a boutonniere. A white sport of this variety, 'Mme. Joseph Schwartz,' was released in 1880 and is equally valuable. It has pink tints on the edges of the petals. We have found both forms of this rose on old sites in Texas and the South. A large specimen of 'Mme. Joseph Schwartz' adorns the front landscape of a New Braunfels, Texas, home and is known by its owner as the "Wedding Rose."

'Duchesse de Brabant'

'Catherine Mermet'

'CATHERINE MERMET'

(kah tuh *reen* mehr *may*)
1869   3'–4'

This is one of the best Teas for cut flower use. Healthy and flowering profusely in our summer heat, 'Catherine Mermet' bears large, pink blossoms all during the warm seasons.

'MARIE VAN HOUTTE'

1871   4'–6'

'Marie van Houtte' epitomizes the distinctive, subtle color combinations that can occur in old Tea Roses. The flowers are large, globular, and lemon yellow. The color is deeper in the center with pinkish-lilac tips washing the edges of the petals. The foliage is a rich, dark green that contrasts well with the light-colored flowers.

'PERLE DES JARDINS'

(pehrl day zhar *dehn*)
1874   3'–5'

The canary-yellow flowers are large, full, and well-formed. Stems are stronger than on most Teas, which made 'Perle des Jardins' one of the most popular cut roses of its time. The foliage has an interesting, slightly crinkled appearance, and new shoots are plum-colored. This rose has been found in a number of old gardens and is among the best yellow roses.

'GENERAL SCHABLIKINE'

1878   3'–5'

Salmon-beige flowers with outer petals edged in carmine appear continuously from spring until fall on one of the finest of all Teas. This rose is said to have better cold resistance than most in its class.

'MADAME LOMBARD'

1878   4'–6'

Large, very double, and fragrant flowers of rosy-salmon have made 'Madame Lombard' a favorite in the South for more than a hundred years. 'Madame Lombard' performs especially well in the cool of October and November, when the color is particularly intense.

'Monsieur Tillier'

'MONSIEUR TILLIER'

1891   3'–6'

Full, fragrant flowers occur throughout the growing season on fairly compact plants. The most distinctive characteristic of this rose is its color: carmine, fading to brick red. Even fully open flowers are more striking than those of most Teas.

'MAMAN COCHET'

1893   3'–4'

'Maman Cochet' is an excellent cut flower having strong stems and a classic, long-budded form. Flowers are a soft pink and fragrance is violet-like. Thorns are few and disease resistance is good. The plant is smaller than most Tea Roses, which makes it useful in compact spaces.

'Souvenir de Madame Leonie Viennot'

'Souvenir de Mme. Leonie Viennot'

1898   15'–20'

This spectacular climber was found by Pamela Puryear of Navasota and given the study name "Climbing Lady Pamela" by her cohorts. After extensive research, it was finally identified as 'Souvenir de Mme. Leonie Viennot.' Pink flowers with creamy yellow centers literally cover the vigorous canes in spring. The plant blooms throughout the season, but later flowerings cannot compare with its spring show.

'Mrs. B. R. Cant'

'Mrs. B. R. Cant'

1901   5'–7'

This is the most prolifically flowering and vigorous Tea Rose I have grown. The large flowers have pale, silver-rose petals tipped with dark rose. They are very full, quartered, and fragrant. It has good resistance to black spot, but some temporary attacks of mildew may occur. 'Mrs. B. R. Cant' is among the best old roses for cutting. My first plant of this rose was a gift from Josephine Kennedy of Springfield, Louisiana. It is a favorite of hers—and of everyone else I know who has grown it.

'Niles Cochet'

1906   3'–4'

'Niles Cochet' is a sport of the famous 'Maman Cochet' and is sometimes known as "Red Maman Cochet." It is a large flowering Tea with long pointed buds of cherry red. The plant is more compact than most Teas, but it's a healthy plant with few thorns.

'Mrs. Dudley Cross'   'Lady Hillingdon'   "McClinton Tea"

'Mrs. Dudley Cross'

1907   4'–6'

This is a favorite of Tea Rose connoisseurs. The full, pale yellow flowers are usually tinged with pink. Stems are thornless or nearly so and the foliage is exceptionally healthy and disease resistant. Color and flower shape are somewhat similar to those of the more modern 'Peace' rose, but 'Mrs. Dudley Cross' is smaller and daintier in size. This is one of the Tea Roses most often found thriving in old or abandoned gardens, especially in San Antonio and south central Texas. The flowers are excellent for cutting.

'Lady Hillingdon'

1910   4'–6'

The beautifully pointed buds of rich apricot-yellow and the young purple shoots and foliage are distinctive features of this lovely rose, and the sepals' ornamented edges add a note of elegance. Flowers are semi-double and occur throughtout the growing season. The plant is less disease resistant than most Teas and not as vigorous, but the apricot blooms set it apart from other Teas. 'Lady Hillingdon' is occasionally found in old gardens.

'Rosette Delizy'

(roh *zeht* duh lee *zee*)
1922   3'–4'

The small but perfectly formed flowers are an ochre yellow edged with brick red. Although a latecomer to the Tea class, 'Rosette Delizy' is distinctive and vigorous but compact and modest in size.

"McClinton Tea"

a found rose   6'–8'

I discovered this rose in the cottage garden of Mrs. McClinton in Natchitoches, Louisiana, during the Christmas season several years ago. It ranks among the very best roses I grow. Flowers are bright pink, semi-double, and very heavily scented with what I consider typical Tea fragrance. The reverse of the petals is much darker than the inside. The plant can be slow to get established but soon becomes a large and beautiful specimen that has excellent disease resistance. There is speculation from research that the true identity of this rose is 'Papa Gontier' (1883), but the only reference to scent I find for 'Papa Gontier' is in Peter Beales's book *Classic Roses* (Henry Holt & Co., 1985), where he describes it as "slightly scented." "McClinton Tea" perfumed the entire front garden where I collected it and has done the same in mine.

Early Hybrid Teas

Eʀʟʏ crosses between Teas and Hybrid Perpetuals resulted in the first Hybrid Teas. 'La France,' introduced in 1867, is considered the first Hybrid Tea Rose. When Hybrid Teas were introduced, the public became fascinated with their high pointed buds and by the 1890s were beginning to prefer them to the flat, open shapes of the older roses.

As *R. foetida* was brought into the breeding, new yellow, red, and orange colors were added. *R. foetida* is also credited with high susceptibility to black spot disease, which has made the class more vulnerable to that major fungal problem. The Tea Roses used in the breeding contributed disease resistance and repeat flowering.

Excessive inbreeding for special colors and flower forms resulted in loss of disease resistance and plant form until recent years; breeders are now trying to repair the damage. A few Hybrid Teas have stood the test of time and are included here for your consideration.

'La France'

'Lᴀ Fʀᴀɴᴄᴇ'

1867   5'–6'

'La France,' the very first Hybrid Tea, has the classic long-pointed bud typical of its Tea ancestry. The fragrant flowers are silvery-pink with darker reverse. There is a swirling characteristic to the center petals that is distinctive to 'La France.' The plant is vigorous, although it is susceptible to black spot in some locations.

'Lᴀᴅʏ Wᴀᴛᴇʀʟᴏᴡ'

1903   10'–12'

Large, semi-double flowers of soft pink with deeper undertones adorn this vigorous climber. Foliage is bold, healthy, and ample. 'Lady Waterlow' is a favorite of old rose expert Ruth Knopf of Edgemoor, South Carolina, who lists it among her favorites for its graceful blooms and free-flowering characteristics.

'Belle Portugaise' makes a romantic drape over a trellis.

'BELLE PORTUGAISE'

(Belle of Portugal)
1903   15'–20'

'Belle Portugaise' is a rose that can create memorable scenes. It is speculated to be a cross between R. *gigantea* and possibly 'Reine Marie Henriette.' The slightly crinkled foliage and long arching canes grow quickly and bloom magnificently for several weeks each spring with large, loosely semi-double flowers of shell pink. 'Belle Portugaise' has naturalized in parts of California and thrives along the Gulf Coast despite damage from hard freezes. This is one of the most cold tender roses I have grown, and it has been severely damaged several times in our area during the past ten years. Suzanne Turner and Scott Purdin have a traffic-stopping specimen covering a trellis at their Victorian home in Baton Rouge, Louisiana.

'Belle Portugaise'

'Radiance'

'Red Radiance'

'Lafter'

'RADIANCE'

1908   4'–6'

This is a famous rose bred by John Cook of Baltimore in 1904 and introduced by Peter Henderson in 1908. This original form is a warm pink in color. Although there are only about two dozen petals, the flowers are large, rounded, and impressive, as well as very fragrant. 'Radiance' is one of the most popular roses of this century and well worth having, if a good, vigorous clone is available.

'RED RADIANCE'

1916   4'–6'

A sport of 'Radiance' that is dark rose, not red, in color, this rose is very similar to its parent in every way except in color, and it probably became even more popular.

'CLIMBING ETOILE DE HOLLAND'

1931   10'–12'

Well-formed, fragrant blooms of about thirty-five petals and unfading scarlet-crimson color make 'Climbing Etoile de Holland' one of the most popular roses of all time. Flowers can sometimes measure five to six inches across. This is a climbing sport of the bush form which was introduced in 1919.

'CRIMSON GLORY'

1935   5'–6'

A Wilhelm Kordes introduction, 'Crimson Glory' is the red rose to which all others are compared. It is a deep, velvety maroon-red with petals of excellent substance and unforgettable fragrance. 'Climbing Crimson Glory' was introduced in 1946 and quickly became one of the nation's most popular roses.

'LAFTER'

1948   6'–8'

My plant of 'Lafter' was a gift from Dr. Robert Basye, who considers it to be one of the most black spot-resistant and vigorous roses he has grown. It has become over eight feet tall and is an upright-rounded, healthy shrub with rich, green foliage. Flowers are a blend of salmon-pink, apricot, and a touch of yellow. They are semi-double and fragrant. Stems are very thorny, and rebloom is not as consistent as in most others in the class. 'Lafter' is an ideal hedge rose.

Bourbons

Bourbon Roses resulted from a natural cross between 'Old Blush' and 'Autumn Damask,' both planted as hedges on the French island then called Bourbon and now called Reunion. An alert resident sent the plant to France, where breeders further perfected the class. The first cultivar was painted by Redoute in 1817. There are about forty varieties still in commerce today.

Bourbons have some of the most beautiful flowers ever developed. They often have old-fashioned cupped or quartered blossoms, generally in pastel pinks, on large, robust plants. Due to their Damask influence, Bourbons tend to be more cold hardy than Chinas or Teas. Only a few varieties reliably repeat-flower in summer and fall in the South. These roses also tend to be more susceptible to black spot and mildew than Chinas or Teas. Bourbon flowers tend to be highly fragrant and beautifully formed, which accounts for their popularity in spite of their spray requirements and sometimes sparse bloom.

'Souvenir de la Malmaison'

'SOUVENIR DE LA MALMAISON'

(soov *nihr*'d la mahl meh *zohn*)
1843   3'–4'

Many knowledgeable old rose collectors consider this to be far and away the finest Bourbon Rose ever created. Malmaison was Empress Josephine's country estate outside Paris. This rose did not grow there amid her fine collection but was introduced after her death and named in honor of her garden. 'Souvenir de la Malmaison' produces large, flat, quartered blossoms with thick petals, in a beautiful tint of pink. Fragrance is fine and the bush tends to be compact and attractive. It is the most reliably repeat-flowering Bourbon I have grown, and the only one I have found surviving in old Southern gardens. Thomas Affleck, the great nurseryman and writer, said of 'Souvenir de la Malmaison' in 1856, "How I envy the grower who first saw that plant bloom, the seed of which he had sown, feeling that such a gem was his!"

'Kronprinzessin Viktoria'

'Louise Odier'

'Zéphirine Drouhin'

'Zéphirine Drouhin' is a popular wall rose in England.

Texas rose rustlers first found this rose in Anderson, Texas, at the home of Mary Minor. After researching the find for many months, we finally agreed that we had found the famous 'Souvenir de la Malmaison.' In 1983, while searching for roses in Brenham, we came across what appeared to be a very similar rose except that it was pure white, at the home of Mrs. Carl Meyer. This rose was later identified as 'Kronprinzessin Viktoria,' the white sport of 'Souvenir' that was released in 1888. It is even more compact growing than the mannerly 'Souvenir' and rarely exceeds two to three feet.

The climbing sport of 'Souvenir de la Malmaison' was introduced in 1893 and appears to have the good qualities of the bush type in the climbing form.

'LOUISE ODIER'

1851   4'–6'

The very full, medium sized, camellia-shaped blooms are a beautiful tint of light rose or deep pink inside. They have a delightful fragrance but rebloom only infrequently after the first long and impressive show in spring. Greg Grant has found what appears to be a very old plant of 'Louise Odier' growing unattended in a San Antonio garden. His find fits the descriptions perfectly but tends to rebloom much better than the nursery-grown plants I have purchased.

'ZÉPHIRINE DROUHIN'

(zah fih *reen* droo *ehn*)
1868   6'–15'

This mannerly climber is a treasure in the garden for its unusual, semi-double, cerise flowers and thornless stems. It is sometimes used as a large shrub and is one of the most popular wall roses in England. It has done beautifully in my Texas garden and finally, several years after planting, offers a few fall flowers in addition to a magnificent show in the spring. It is very fragrant and moderately disease resistant.

'MME. ISAAC PEREIRE'

(pehr *rehr*)
1881   6'–7'

This is a very full and sumptuous rose. The flowers are subtle, bright rose madder with perhaps the strongest rose perfume extant. The plant is vigorous and thorny but quite susceptible to black spot. Although it is described as a good fall bloomer in the literature, like many of the Bourbons grown in the deep South, it rarely flowers after a long and plentiful spring season.

'MME. ERNST CALVAT'

1888   5'–7'

Actually a sport of 'Mme. Isaac Pereire,' 'Mme. Ernst Calvat' produces dozens of quartered, full, rich pink flowers each spring. It may be grown as a shrub or trained on a wall, pillar, or fence.

'VARIEGATA DI BOLOGNA'

1909   4'–7'

The distinctively striped flowers of 'Variegata di Bologna' make it a popular choice in the garden or for cut flowers in the home. The very round flowers are three to four inches across and appear in clusters of three to five. The white blossoms are streaked, flecked, and splashed with pale purple and are well-scented.

"MAGGIE"

a found rose

This was the first old garden rose I found and propagated. During the Christmas season of 1980 I decided to take cuttings of a rose that seemed always to be in bloom at my wife's grandmother's farm near Mangham, Louisiana. The flowers are very full and highly fra-

'Mme. Isaac Pereire'

'Variegata di Bologna'

"Maggie"

grant, and an interesting scent of black pepper lingers on the hand that picks a bloom or handles its stems.

I took cuttings of "Maggie" and also another interesting rose growing nearby that we later identified as the 'Swamp Rose,' wrapped them carefully in moist paper towels, and placed them in a plastic bag. After several days in the bag, the cuttings were stuck in an east-facing flower bed in our College Station garden. They rooted and began blooming later that spring. They have grown vigorously and were shared with the Antique Rose Emporium, the Huntington Botanical Garden, and Joyce Demits of Heritage Roses in Ft. Bragg, California.

Since growing and propagating "Maggie" for some ten years, we have found it in numerous old gardens and cemeteries. Sometimes it is trained as a climber, but most often as a large bush. It seems odd that a rose so fine and popular is still unidentified. It has been speculated to be 'Grüss an Teplitz,' but there are definite differences in the foliage and vigor as well as in the flowers. More recent research has indicated the possibility that "Maggie" may be 'Eugene E. Marlitt,' but I find it questionable that a rose as fine as this would be so obscure in the literature. Whatever its true identity, "Maggie" must have a healthy dose of China Rose in its parentage, since it blooms as often and long as any China in my garden. It also propagates easily from cuttings, which helps explain its popularity among rural gardeners of the South.

Hybrid Perpetuals

T HE Hybrid Perpetual class contains some of the most beautiful flowers ever developed. Typically, they are very large, full, and heavily scented. The bushes tend to be tall and sometimes ungainly, but they can be shaped to become usable landscape plants. Some of the Hybrid Perpetuals are outstanding cut flowers.

The "perpetual" part of the name is something of a misnomer. It was wishful thinking on the part of the Victorians who developed these roses, for they are remontant rather than perpetual. Most varieties bloom heavily in spring, rest during summer, then bear scattered flowers in fall. The class has been interbred with almost all types of garden roses, but is perhaps closest to the Bourbons and Damasks.

Hybrid Perpetuals were forerunners of the modern Hybrid Teas and have some similar characteristics. They are not as disease resistant as the Teas and Chinas but probably are less prone to black spot and mildew than the Bourbons.

An interesting way to grow Hybrid Perpetuals is to "peg" them. One method of pegging is to fasten the ends of the canes to the ground with stakes or wire pins; the lateral buds will break from the canes and provide a beautiful fountain effect. Another form of pegging is to secure all the canes as closely as possible to the ground, so that the plant actually becomes a ground cover. The most popular way to grow Hybrid Perpetuals is as chunky shrubs with little trimming.

'Rose du Roi'

'ROSE DU ROI'

1815   3′–4′

'Rose du Roi' is sometimes classified as a Portland and is an important rose. Typical of the Portland Roses, the flowers are nestled in the foliage in a way somewhat resembling a nosegay. They are large, opening quartered into a flat bloom with a green button center covered by petals. Color is bright red, shaded violet. 'Rose du Roi' reblooms well and the flowers are highly scented. The stems have few thorns and foliage is pointed, crinkled, and dark green.

'ROSE DE RESCHT'

date of origin unknown   3'

Although its origins are unknown, 'Rose de Rescht' is sometimes classed with the Portlands or Hybrid Perpetuals. Its flowers are rich fuschia-red with purple overtones. They are highly fragrant and rebloom well in the South. Peter Beales, in *Classic Roses*, suggests that after a plant of 'Rose de Rescht' reaches five years old it sometimes loses its tendency to rebloom. This he says can be easily overcome by harsh pruning.

'MARQUISE BOCELLA'

1842   3'–5'

This rose is sometimes listed in the Portland class, of which there are few remaining members. It is also known as "Jacques Cartier" by some authorities. By any name or class, it is one of the finest old roses available, blooming almost constantly with medium-sized, button-eyed, bright pink powder-puff flowers. The blooms have numerous tiny petals which reflex to give this charming effect. One blossom's light, sweet, Damask fragrance can fill a room. 'Marquise Bocella' is among the easiest and most rewarding of the old roses to grow, but it does not like alkaline soils. It is a very distinctive flower and plant that, once grown, is never forgotten.

'BARONNE PREVOST'

1842   4'–5'

The large, flat blooms of 'Baronne Prevost' appear most of the year in considerable profusion. Although highly susceptible to black spot fungus, the plant seems to be sufficiently vigorous to withstand the attacks. Flowers are a rich pink and appear at the terminals of rather long, thorny canes.

'GÉANT DES BATAILLES'

(zhay *ahn* day bah *ty*)
1846   4'–6'

This has been one of the best rebloomers in my garden but also one that is very susceptible to black spot. 'Giant of Battles' produces flowers of medium size in a beautiful red-purple color. They are highly fragrant and recurrent and produce a handsome shrub useful in borders or mass plantings.

'GENERAL JACQUEMINOT'

(zhay nay *rahl* zhock mee *noh*)
1853   4'–6'

Known affectionately as "General Jack," this rose was immensely popular for many years and was used in the breeding of many later roses. The dark red flowers have good fragrance and were among the first to be sold commercially as cut flowers.

'COMTE DE CHAMBORD'

1860   3'–4'

The highly double flowers of this rose are bright pink fading to lilac-mauve. They have the typical fine fragrance of the Portland Roses. The bush is compact and flowers occur over a long season. It is a very elegant rose and a favorite of many rose growers.

'REINE DES VIOLETTES'

1860   4'–5'

Of 'Queen of the Violets' British rose expert Peter Beales says, "If I had to choose just one Hybrid Perpetual, it would have to be this one." Houston area rose expert Marion Brandes says, "Super in its first year. Bloomed two or three cycles in spring—early summer

'Rose de Rescht'

'Marquise Boccella'

'Géant des Batailles'

'General Jacqueminot'

'Comte de Chambord'

'Reine des Violettes'

'Baroness Rothschild'

'Souvenir du Docteur Jamain'

'Paul Neyron'

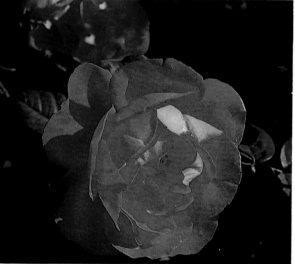

'Ulrich Brünner Fils'

'Climbing American Beauty'

and again in fall. Beautiful, unique matt green foliage that is vigorous and healthy." The shrub is upright growing and almost thornless. Flowers of soft violet open flat and quartered, but shatter quickly. Fragrance is outstanding.

'Souvenir du Docteur Jamain'

(soov *nihr* doo doc *tuhr* zhah *mehn*)
1865   5'–6'

The neat blooms of this rose are sometimes quartered and other times open centered. The crimson-maroon color ages to almost purple and is truly distinctive, as is the fragrance. Ancestry is legendary and includes the famed 'General Jacqueminot' (1853), 'Victory Verdier' (1859), and 'La Reine' (1843).

'Baroness Rothschild'

1868   4'–6'

This rose was introduced by the famous French firm of Pernet and has huge blooms of light pink with exceptional fragrance. The flowers are of the cabbage type and cupped.

'Paul Neyron'

(pohl nay *rohn*)
1869   5'–6'

The huge, fragrant, rose-pink flowers often reach six to seven inches in diameter and are the epitome of old rose blossoms for many people. With its thornless stems and attractive foliage, a good flower of 'Paul Neyron' is a joy to behold. It has rebloomed well in my garden during all but the very hottest time of the summer and is a personal favorite. This rose has often been referred to as a "cabbage rose." Fully opened flowers resemble large peonies and last well as cut flowers.

'American Beauty'

1875   4'–5'

'American Beauty' is a legendary rose. It is remembered for its name and the dark, rich, pink color of its blossoms. The three- to four-inch globular blooms have excellent substance and a strong, heavy rose scent. The stems have few thorns and the plant tends to rebloom well. 'American Beauty' was developed as a greenhouse rose for cut flower production. It does not perform as well in the garden as most of the other Hybrid Perpetuals I grow, but its blooms are beautiful and its place in history secure.

'Climbing American Beauty'

1909   12'–15'

This deep-rose, large-flowered climber is not a sport but a result of a series of crosses between 'American Beauty,' the species *R. wichuraiana*, and a Hybrid Tea. Still found in some of the old gardens of Texas and the South, it is spectacular in spring but has not rebloomed in my garden.

'Ulrich Brünner Fils'

1881   4'–6'

This has been one of the most profusely flowering and dependable rebloomers of all the Hybrid Perpetuals I have grown. The flowers are large and fairly full in an intense bright rose-red on a big, healthy bush. Fragrance is good, and the size and form of the plant make it useful as a hedge or specimen.

'Frau Karl Druschki'

'MARCHIONESS OF LONDONDERRY'

1893   5'–6'

The flowers of this variety are often referred to as "cabbage roses." Actually, roses in the Centifolia class correctly carry this title but they do not generally thrive in the deep South. The huge flowers of 'Marchioness of Londonderry' are white, tinged pale pink, and reminiscent of the artificial flowers sometimes found in Victorian millinery.

'FRAU KARL DRUSCHKI'

1901   4'–6'

Better known as "White American Beauty" or "Snow Queen" in the South, this rose was immensely popular during the early twentieth century. The flowers are as pure white as any rose I know and are large, with pointed buds. In spite of its almost total lack of fragrance, 'Frau Karl Druschki' is a wonderful rose for garden or vase.

Polyanthas

Polyantha Roses were created by crossing the Chinas with the rambling Japanese Multiflora Rose. The Chinas gave their everblooming characteristic and shrub shape to some of the roses in this class. Since both parents were from the same area in the Far East, some Polyanthas occurred naturally.

After the importation of the Multiflora Rose into France in the early 1860s, work began to create roses that could be massed for borders and other landscape applications. The result was a group of roses that bloomed prolifically, were compact in size, and had large clusters of relatively small flowers. Fragrance varies from almost nonexistent to some of the finest ever created.

Polyanthas are excellent for low hedges, mass plantings, and container use. The perfectly formed buds of many of them are ideal for boutonnieres. Although there are exceptions, my experience indicates the earlier members of the class to be more valuable in the garden. Some of the later Polyanthas appear to be highly susceptible to mildew. Most varieties rebloom prolifically throughout the growing season.

'CÉCILE BRÜNNER'

1881   3'–4'

One of the most beloved roses of all time, 'Cécile Brünner' was created in France by Joseph Pernet-Ducher, who crossed 'Mignonette' and a Tea Rose named 'Madame de Tartas.' The flowers are lightly fragrant and are like perfectly formed miniature Teas, the exquisite pink buds opening to 1 1/2-inch reflexed flowers. 'Cécile Brünner' blooms heavily in spring, followed by continuous flowering until freezing weather. It is long-lived and has healthy foliage. Although this rose is often referred to by the masculine name Cecil, research by old rose authorities confirms that it was named for a woman and is properly called Cécile.

'Climbing Cécile Brünner' was introduced in 1894 and is one of the finest climbing roses ever created. It is much more vigorous than the bush form and has a natural umbrella shape. 'Climbing Cécile Brünner' can reach fifteen to twenty feet on a trellis, fence, or wall. I have also seen it growing without support in an umbrella shape eight to ten feet across. Most of the old plants found in cemeteries and gardens are the climbing form, which attests to its unusual stamina and adaptibility to a wide range of growing conditions. Although more spectacular during spring and fall than is the dwarf form, 'Climbing Cécile Brünner' blooms much less during the summer months. Foliage is a rich green and is disease resistant.

'Climbing Cécile Brünner' with shasta daisies

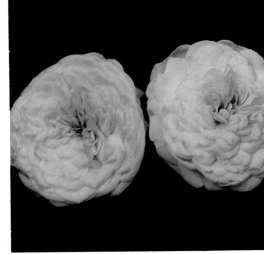

'Perle d'Or'   'Marie Pavié'   'Clotilde Soupert'

'PERLE D'OR'

(pehrl dohr)
1884   3'–4'

This rose is very similar to the dwarf form of 'Cécile Brünner' but with a slightly more salmon to orange-toned bloom. 'Perle d'Or' is lightly fragrant, with beautifully formed buds, and is effective in masses, hedges, and specimen or container plantings. Its color is unique, and the plant is almost always in bloom during the growing season. 'Perle d'Or is exceptionally disease resistant and blooms well in hot weather.

'MARIE PAVIÉ'

(pahv *yay*)
1888   2'–4'

This is one of the most useful roses I know. I obtained my first plant from Claire Martin at the Huntington Botanical Garden in 1983 and was so enthralled with it there that I hand-carried it home and immediately shared it with the Antique Rose Emporium and other nurseries and collectors. Since then we have found it growing on a few old cemeteries and homesites in Texas.

The pale pink buds occur in medium-size clusters and open to semi-double, blush-white flowers. The flowers are intensely fragrant with a wonderful Musk scent, and the stems are usually thornless. Foliage is dark and healthy with small prickles on the underside of the midribs. The plant is occasionally attacked by black spot during the cool season but is usually vigorous enough to overcome it. Blooms occur in abundance all through the warm months. 'Marie Pavié' is a most useful landscape plant, ideal in containers or as a three- to four-foot hedge.

'CLOTILDE SOUPERT'

(kloh *tihld* soo *pehr*)
1890   3'–4'

The individual flowers of 'Clotilde Soupert' are unlike any other Polyantha—large and full, sometimes quartered, with over a hundred neatly layered pale pink petals. Fragrance is outstanding, but mildew and black spot are especially troublesome during spring and fall. The flowers also tend to ball in humid weather.

'Climbing Clotilde Soupert' was introduced in 1902 and has all the desirable characteristics of the bush. Since it is a large-growing climber, problems with disease are somewhat less common.

'La Marne'

"The Fairy" has tiny, double flowers.

'TIP TOP'

1909   3'–4'

'Tip Top' is a favorite of Cleo Barnwell of Shreveport, Louisiana, who has had this rose in her garden for many years, and of Marion Brandes of Houston. The following description comes from Marion Brandes: "A pleasing departure from the usual Polyantha Rose, for its blooms look like miniature Hybrid Tea flowers, and are borne singly. Its color is best described as variegated, for the buds are canary yellow tipped with pale or deer rose, and the inner petals are cream, striped and splashed with pink. It is a moderate grower of dwarf habit and is the very ideal of the sorts called button hole roses." Foliage is healthy.

'LA MARNE'

1915   4'–6'

'La Marne' is an excellent landscape rose, quite effective as a hedge. The ten-petaled flowers with pink edges and cream-white centers are borne in clusters. Specimens of 'La Marne' are fairly common in old cemeteries throughout Texas and the South. Although susceptible to mildew, especially in spring, completely neglected plants often survive and look good for much of the year. The fragrant flowers are at their very best during the cooler parts of the blooming season.

'MEVROUW NATHALIE NYPELS'

1919   2'–3'

'Nathalie Nypels' is very similar to 'La Marne.' The foliage is dark green and glossy. Clusters of loose, semi-double, bright pink flowers occur continuously and are slightly larger than those of 'La Marne.' Fragrance is vague but the flowers and shrub are choice.

'THE FAIRY'

1932   3'–4'

Sprays of tiny, double, rose pink flowers against petite, dark green leaves combine to make 'The Fairy' a tidy, handsome, and useful shrub. Flowering begins later than in most roses, usually by mid-May. Summer heat turns the flowers nearly white, but the blooms continue as long as some moisture is available. Stems are very thorny and the flowers have little fragrance, but the glossy foliage, compact form, and masses of pink blooms ensure the continued popularity of this fine rose. It is excellent for hedges, mass plantings, or container use. Disease resistance is better than that of most roses in its class.

'Climbing Pinkie'

'Jean Mermoz'

1937   1'–2'

The flowers of 'Jean Mermoz' are lasting and of great substance. They occur in clusters of six to nine and are a beautiful, clear pink. Fragrance is minimal, but the compact form and beautiful, long-lasting flowers are sufficient to recommend this rose for low masses and containers.

'China Doll'

1946   12"–18"

'China Doll' blooms later in the spring than most roses and continues to make a good showing until late fall. The 1 1/2-inch double blooms have sixteen to twenty petals and are medium pink. They are cupped and in clusters. 'China Doll' is a good border or edging rose. Its leathery foliage, compact form, disease resistance, and continuous bloom make it a useful landscape plant.

'Climbing Pinkie'

1952   6'–10'

This rose was originally collected by Tommy Adams and given the study name "Seguin College Street Pink." It became an almost instant favorite with many of us who have grown it because of its graceful form, thornless canes, and fountains of fragrant, semi-double flowers of bright pink. Although classified as a climber, 'Climbing Pinkie' is also useful as a large, mounding shrub that requires no support. Disease resistance is good, and its general hardiness and vigor make it one of the best landscape roses I have grown.

"Caldwell Pink"

a found Polyantha   3'–4'

This rose was a gift from Mrs. Webb, who operated a small nursery in Caldwell, Texas, several years ago. It was growing in her garden as a gift from a Somerville friend who had had it in the family for many years. "Caldwell Pink" is a very prolific bloomer throughout the growing season. The double lilac-pink flowers are in clusters on a rather neat and mannerly shrub. The only real fault of this rose is its almost total lack of fragrance. This is somewhat compensated for by its profuse flowering and fall leaf color. It is one of the few roses I have grown that reliably provides red and purple leaf color in October and November each year. I was fascinated to observe that this rose was an exact copy of a climber given to me by Angela and Jerry Fannin from Jerry's grandparents' home in Madisonville, Texas, except that their rampant climber bloomed only in spring, and "Caldwell Pink" reblooms all season and is a bush. Some experts have speculated that the correct identity may be 'Pink Pet.'

Hybrid Musks

THE Hybrid Musks include some of the most useful roses for landscape purposes. The first varieties were created by the Reverend Joseph Hardwick Pemberton (1850–1926), an East Anglian cleric who bred a possible hybrid of *Rosa moschata* with certain Hybrid Teas and Polyanthas to establish this distinctive rose class. The Reverend Mr. Pemberton bequeathed all his stock and seedlings to John and Ann Bentall, his gardeners. The Bentalls released some of Pemberton's roses as well as others they themselves bred and raised.

In the South, the Hybrid Musks tend to bloom heavily in the spring, followed by scattered summer flowers and some fall flowering, although all varieties do not put on a good fall show. Hybrid Musks may be used as shrubs, mannerly climbers, pillars, or hedges. The colors are beautiful pastels and blends, the fragrance outstanding, foliage handsome, and disease resistance good. Some varieties even bear handsomely ornamental fruit. In addition to being long-lived and easily grown, Hybrid Musks reportedly tolerate more shade than most roses.

'Aglaia'

'AGLAIA'

1896   8'–10'

This rose is also known as "Yellow Rambler." 'Aglaia' and 'Trier' are significant because of their role as parents for many of the roses Pemberton raised. The small, pale yellow 'Aglaia' flowers occur in clusters on almost thornless stems. Foliage is bright green with bronzy tints. 'Aglaia' is useful as a climber or shrub.

'TRIER'

1904   5'–7'

This white rambling rose is important as one of the ancestors of Pemberton's and Bentall's Hybrid Musks. 'Trier' is lax in growth habit with small, blush-white blossoms showing yellow at the base of each petal. The small, red fruit is plentiful and attractive. 'Trier' is outstanding trained on a pillar or as a specimen and is reported to be quite shade tolerant.

'Trier'

'PROSPERITY'

1919   4'–6'

Dark green foliage and sweetly fragrant, double flowers of ivory white with touches of pink describe this versatile plant. One of the few Hybrid Musks found in old Texas and Southern gardens, 'Prosperity' is sometimes trained as a climber. Red fruits provide an extra color accent. 'Prosperity' is one of the best Hybrid Musks for fall bloom.

'VANITY'

1920   8'–10'

Cerise-pink flowers recur throughout the season on this beautiful and unusual shrub of lax habit that often spreads as wide as it is tall. The cerise-pink color is striking in the garden and useful as a background for perennials or lower, more compact-growing roses or shrubs. Fall brings large, orange hips, which are judged the best in the class by some experts. 'Vanity' is one of the few roses that is noticed in the garden even if it has only two or three open flowers. 'Vanity' also tends to be more shade tolerant than most Hybrid Musks.

'NUR MAHAL'

1923   5'–6'

English rose authority Peter Beales says there is much to commend 'Nur Mahal.' Its foliage is especially luxuriant, and the well-scented bright crimson, semi-double flowers are bright and showy in the garden. 'Nur Mahal' is another introduction of Mr. Pemberton's.

'PENELOPE'

1924   4'–5'

The most popular of the Pemberton Musks, 'Penelope' is a dense, twiggy bush reaching five feet high and even wider than it is tall. Vigorous and large-leaved, it bears dense corymbs of very pale salmon-pink flowers of strong aroma, followed by a winter crop of unusual pink hips. It is excellent as a hedge or shrub. 'Penelope' is a good fall bloomer.

'CORNELIA'

1925   5'–6'

'Cornelia' has a subtle scent and a luscious color unique among the Hybrid Musks. The flowers are small, semi-double, and pale coral with gold stamens that show well against the dark green foliage. It is useful as a large shrub, specimen, or easily managed climber.

'BISHOP DARLINGTON'

1926   4'–6'

Coral-pink buds open to large, creamy, semi-double flowers imbued with true Musk fragrance. An upright form makes 'Bishop Darlington' useful for hedges.

'FELICIA'

1928   4'–6'

Apricot-pink, very double flowers that lighten to cream and salmon adorn this moderate-size shrub. The foliage is very dark green and slightly crinkled at the edges. 'Felicia' is one of the best fall blooming Hybrid Musks.

'AUTUMN DELIGHT'

1933   5'–6'

After the Reverend Mr. Pemberton's death, his nursery manager, John A. Bentall, introduced this and other roses based on his breeding. 'Autumn Delight' is almost single-flowered. The large, spectacular blooms are off-white and have prominent stamens.

'Prosperity'

'Vanity'

'Penelope' forms a dense, twiggy bush.

'Penelope'

'Cornelia'

'Skyrocket' can be a massive bush.

'Skyrocket'

'Belinda'

'SKYROCKET'

1934   4'–6'

'Skyrocket' blooms in flushes with huge clusters of true red flowers—an unusual color for the class—covering a husky plant that can reach six feet tall and wide. It is one of the few Hybrid Musks found in Southern gardens, although there is some question about its true identity. 'Skyrocket' was created by Wilhelm Kordes of Germany.

'BELINDA'

1936   4'–8'

This is a latter-day Hybrid Musk introduced by Ann Bentall. 'Belinda' matures into a rounded bush bearing fragrant, soft pink flowers with a white eye and about ten petals each. It repeats well and bears clusters of red fruit. When at their peak of spring bloom, the flower clusters remind me of hydrangeas.

'BALLERINA'

1937   4'–6'

'Ballerina' originated as a chance seedling discovered by Ann Bentall. An outstanding landscape plant with dense, healthy, vigorous growth, 'Ballerina' lends itself especially well to group or mass plantings. The small, single flowers are light pink with white eyes and occur in large clusters throughout the growing season. The small fruits resemble nandina berries and are probably the most ornamental in the class. Mounded form and fountain-like character make 'Ballerina' an unusually attractive and useful plant. Stems do not appear very thorny, but are particularly sharp and bothersome to work around.

'BUFF BEAUTY'

1939   4'–6'

The two-inch blooms of 'Buff Beauty' are muted apricot that blends beautifully with other old rose pastels. Its habit is a spreading bush, and its unbelievable flush of spring and fall bloom make it a favorite in the class. Like most other Hybrid Musks, 'Buff Beauty' is a shy bloomer the first year it is planted and tends to increase in floral display each year.

'ERFURT'

1939   4'–6'

The deep rose-colored, semi-double blooms are creamy white at the base of the petals and have prominent gold stamens and a strong musk fragrance. This cascading bush reblooms well.

'Ballerina'

'Ballerina' has a fountain-like character.

'Buff Beauty'

'Erfurt'

'Will Scarlet'

'Lavender Lassie'

'WIND CHIMES'

circa 1949   6′–7′

Single, rosy-pink flowers paling toward the center in large sprays, followed by red fruit, characterize this later addition to the Hybrid Musk class. Fragrance is good and the plant is vigorous and thorny.

'LAVENDER LASSIE'

1960   10′–12′

'Lavender Lassie' is a beautiful tint of lilac-purple. The semi-double, fragrant flowers are produced in large, showy clusters. It was introduced by Wilhelm Kordes of Germany. Like many of the Hybrid Musks, 'Lavender Lassie' may be trained as a shrub or a climber. A climbing specimen seen at the Huntington Botanical Garden in 1983 remains a vivid memory.

'WILL SCARLET'

1948   5′–7′

A sport of 'Skyrocket,' 'Will Scarlet' produces abundant clusters of medium-sized, fragrant flowers intermittently through the growing season, followed by profuse quantities of medium-sized, orange-red fruit. The scarlet flowers make 'Will Scarlet' a popular choice among those seeking a good low-maintenance shrub or climber.

Shrub and Climbing Roses from Assorted Classes

THIS section includes a potpourri of roses worthy of consideration as shrubs and climbers in the South. Some are relatively modern, while others have been mainstays over many years. While fragrance and beauty of individual flowers is considered, the main value of these roses is their contribution to the landscape. Sometimes just the addition of a few climbers and larger shrub roses can change the entire feeling of a garden.

'HARISON'S YELLOW'

Hybrid Foetida
1830   6′–10′

Pioneers moving westward often took 'Harison's Yellow' with them, and it persists in old California gardens today, testifying to the transcontinental trek to new frontiers. Some historians consider 'Harison's Yellow' to be the "Yellow Rose of Texas." The semi-double flowers are a deep, pure, golden yellow with golden stamens. The shrub is thorny with dark green foliage. George F. Harison was a New York lawyer and amateur rosarian who apparently bred this rose in a suburban garden and sold it to a retailer, who popularized it. Spring blooming only, it is better adapted to areas at least one to two hundred miles inland from the Gulf Coast. 'Harison's Yellow' is drought tolerant and disease resistant in areas where it thrives.

'MAY QUEEN'

Wichuraiana rambler
1898   12′–15′

The lilac-pink semi-double flowers of 'May Queen' occur over a fairly long period in spring. They are fragrant and appear in clusters on vigorous stems with dark green foliage.

'Harison's Yellow'

'Grüss an Aachen' in a parterre at Tudor Place in the Georgetown area of Washington, D.C.

'Evangeline'

'Silver Moon'

'EVANGELINE'

Walsh rambler
1906   12'–15'

Clusters of single, pale pink flowers appear in tremendous profusion late in spring. A huge specimen of this rose was in full bloom in Miriam Wilkins's California garden when I visited there in 1983. When she visited Texas in the spring of 1989 Miriam brought me a cutting which is now rooted and ready to plant in our country garden this spring.

'GRÜSS AN AACHEN'

Floribunda
1909   3'–4'

'Grüss an Aachen' is generally considered to be the first Floribunda Rose, and by some to be the best of the class. The flat three-inch flowers are a beautiful shell pink tinted with salmon. The bush is compact growing and replenishes itself constantly with the beautiful and fragrant blooms.

'SILVER MOON'

Wichuraiana rambler
1910   10'–20'

'Silver Moon' is a vigorous, healthy, once-blooming rose that may be used as a large mound or climber. The foliage is a dark, shiny green and the flowers are loose, semi-double, pure white with showy yellow stamens. It is very thorny but also nicely fragrant. 'Silver Moon' can sometimes be found surviving in old gardens.

'BABY FAURAX'

parentage unknown
1924   1'–2'

English rosarian Jack Harkness describes 'Baby Faurax' as having small, very double, fragrant flowers of dark amethyst. There is a touch of white in the centers and the yellow stamens are prominent. Speculation is that there is R. *multiflora* in its background; perhaps it is the dwarf form of a Multiflora rambler. It is a good specimen for pot culture or a low hedge and the color is very unusual.

'MARY WALLACE'

Wichuraiana rambler
1924   8'–10'

'Mary Wallace' is a warm pink rambler with semi-double flowers of excellent scent that appear rather late in spring. Bred by Fleet in the United States, 'Mary Wallace' is a cross between R. *wichuraiana* and an unknown pink Hybrid Tea. It has an upright form and may be used as a shrub or climber.

'MME. GREGOIRE STAECHELIN'

large-flowered climber
1927   12'–15'

Another name for this climbing rose of unusual vigor is 'Spanish Beauty.' Flowers are large and pale pink with deeper coloring on the reverses of the petals. It flowers early and repeats later in the season. If the spent flowers are not removed, it will set handsome orange-red hips that ripen in the fall. While I was visiting Kew Gardens several years ago a specimen of 'Mme. Gregoire Staechelin' was in full bloom on one of the pergola structures. It was among the earliest roses in flower and surely among the most beautiful. It originated in Spain as a cross between 'Frau Karl Druschki' and 'Chateau de Clos Vougeot.'

'Mary Wallace'

'Baby Faurax'

'Mme. Gregoire Staechlin'

'BLAZE'

climber
1932   7'–9'

'Blaze' is reported to be the descendant of a cross between 'Paul's Scarlet Climber' and 'Grüss an Teplitz.'
Medium-red flowers are semi-double with eighteen to
twenty-four petals and are about three inches across.
The cupped flowers occur in clusters throughout the
growing seasons. Good clones of this rose are reported
to be disease resistant. 'Blaze' is a very popular rose in
the South because it is so free-flowering and readily
available.

'BETTY PRIOR'

Floribunda
1935   3'–5'

'Betty Prior' is a single rose of rich pink and good fragrance. It blooms prolifically during the warm seasons
and is reported to be one of the most cold hardy roses.
'Betty Prior' is a good choice for a low hedge and has
remained popular through the years.

'NEW DAWN'

Wichuraiana rambler
1930   15'–20'

'New Dawn' claims the distinction of being U.S. Plant
Patent No. 1, the first rose patented under federal regu-
lations. It is an everblooming sport of the well known
'Dr. W. Van Fleet' and exceeded the popularity of its
parent. The foliage is dark, shiny green, typical of
R. wichuraiana hybrids. Flowers are pale pink and
fairly double. Although considered an everblooming
rose, it tends to bloom heavily in spring, to rest during
the summer, and to repeat with a good fall show. A massive grower, 'New Dawn' is useful as a large hedge or
climber.

'Meg'

'LEVERKUSEN'

hybrid of *Rosa kordesii*
1954   8'–10'

Bright lemon-yellow flowers are semi-double with attractive ragged edges to the petals. 'Leverkusen' continues to bloom throughout the summer and has good
fragrance. The foliage, like the rose, is distinctive,
having deeply serrated margins on the glossy, light
green leaves. To quote Peter Beales, "As so often with
the Kordes roses, rudely healthy."

'MEG'

large-flowered climber
1954   10'–12'

The color of this rose is hard to describe. Flowers begin
as pale salmon-apricot and fade to a blush pink with
some hints of peachy pink. They have wavy petals, are
single or semi-double, and may measure five inches
across. Stamens are prominent and reddish-orange in
color. Foliage is exceptionally healthy. 'Meg' sometimes reblooms modestly after the big spring flush. It is
a beautiful rose to train on a wall or into a tree.

'DORTMUND'

hybrid of R. *kordesii*
1955   6'–8'

'Dortmund' is a spectacular rose. Its large, single crimson flowers contrast with a white eye and yellow stamens. The plant is large and thorny with dark green foliage. 'Dortmund' will rebloom if the old blossoms are removed. If not, it will ripen a handsome fruit crop.

'BELINDA'S ROSE'

shrub
1967   4'–6'

Dr. Robert Basye modestly said in a letter to me dated January 25, 1987, "Last summer I budded onto R. *fortuniana* a rose I think you should have . . . a cross I made some twenty years ago. The bush is of Hybrid Tea stature, a very prolific everbloomer, and need never be sprayed. I will not describe it further except to say that, after twenty years of observation, I give it very high marks . . ."

The large, double flowers attract immediate attention whether on the bush or in the vase, and they are fragrant as well as visually arresting. I have grown 'Belinda's Rose' on 'Fortuniana' rootstock and as an own-root plant and found it to be slightly more vigorous as a grafted plant, but useful either way. Disease resistance has been very good. Dr. Basye has generously offered propagation material to all who are interested; San Antonio area nurseries as well as the Antique Rose Emporium and others are beginning to grow it. It is named for the daughter of a friend of Dr. Basye's in Caldwell, Texas. I have seen it used effectively as a hedge and as a large, rounded shrub. The many-petaled buds will sometimes ball in humid weather.

'Dortmund'

'Belinda's Rose'

'Gene Boerner'

'GENE BOERNER'

Floribunda
1968   4'–6'

In spite of its relatively modern date, I cannot ignore the beauty and usefulness of this rose. It would be just about perfect if it had more fragrance, but for landscape effect it is as good as any rose I know. Beautiful buds open into large clusters of clear pink roses from mid-spring until freezing weather, and the plant is exceptionally healthy, disease resistant, and vigorous. It is a strong grower and can reach six feet or more in a season. I have grown this rose as a grafted plant and from rooted cuttings, both with success. At one time, 'Gene Boerner' was one of the most popular roses in the South. For landscape use it should still be.

'CANTERBURY'

shrub
1969   4'–6'

This rose is an introduction of David Austin in England. A vigorous grower and dependable recurrent bloomer, it has rosy-pink, semi-double flowers of me-dium size, and very fragrant. It is another good choice for use at the back of the border.

"PETITE PINK SCOTCH"

a found rose
prior to 1949

I first came to know this rose in 1980 when my former professor and friend Dr. Richard Stadtherr at Louisiana State University gave me a gallon size plant and suggested that I try it as a shrub or groundcover in Texas. Dr. Stadtherr had received his original plant from the National Arboretum where it had been tested since 1956 and was considered useful as a bank plant. The original specimen had been found in 1949 by Jackson M. Batchelor, of Willard, North Carolina, growing in the garden of a 1750s plantation on the Cape Fear River, near Wilmington, North Carolina.

The plant is truly distinctive. Although the name given it by the National Arboretum would lead one to believe that it is derived from the Scotch Rose (*Rosa spinosissima*), after observing and researching that group of roses I agree with Charles Walker, president of the Heritage Rose Foundation, who is quite certain that this rose is a hybrid of *R. wichuraiana*. The tiny evergreen leaves form two- to three-inch mounds of cascading branches that are covered with dime-sized, fully double pale pink flowers for several weeks each spring. The tips of the branches root where they touch the ground, making it a good groundcover plant. It is a good idea to prune the plants severely every two or three years to keep them neat. "Petite Pink Scotch" is a very tough plant. It does prefer a neutral to slightly acid soil. For the first several years I grew it there were no insect or disease problems at all, but spider mites later found my plants irresistible. "Petite Pink Scotch" is an unusual rose that is useful on modest slopes.

List of Roses Included in Text

Species and Related Hybrids
'Musk Rose'
'Sweetbrier'
'Swamp Rose'
'Cherokee'
'Virginiana'
'Carnea'
'Lady Banks' Rose'—white
'Lady Banks' Rose'—yellow
'Prairie Rose'
'Chestnut Rose'
'Seven Sisters'
'Russell's Cottage Rose'
'White Carolina Rambler'
'Fortune's Double Yellow'
'Fortuniana'
'Anemone Rose'
'Vielchenblau'
'Mermaid'
'Basye's Purple Rose'
'Memorial Rose'

Chinas
'Old Blush'
'Cramoisi Supérieur'
'Louis Philippe'
'Archduke Charles'
'Hermosa'
'The Green Rose'
'Mutabilis'
'Comtesse du Cayla'
'Ducher'
"Martha Gonzales"
"Highway 290 Pink Buttons"
"Old Gay Hill Red China"
"Pam's Pink"

Noisettes
'Champneys' Pink Cluster'
'Aimée Vibert'
'Lamarque'
'Jaune Desprez'
'Chromatella'
'Jeanne D'Arc'
'Céline Forestier'
'Maréchal Niel'
'Rêve d'Or'
'William Allen Richardson'
'Mme. Alfred Carrière'
'Nastarana'
'Claire Jacquier'
'Mary Washington'
"Natchitoches Noisette"

Old European Roses
'The Apothecary Rose'
'Rosa Mundi'
'Celsiana'
'Autumn Damask'
'Hippolyte'
'Madame Plantier'
'Banshee'
'Salet'
'Deuil de Paul Fontaine'
'Mme. Louis Leveque'

Teas
'Bon Silène'
'Devoniensis'
'Safrano'
'Sombreuil'
'Gloire de Dijon'
'Isabella Sprunt'

'Duchesse de Brabant'
'Catherine Mermet'
'Marie van Houtte'
'Perle des Jardins'
'General Schablikine'
'Madame Lombard'
'Monsieur Tillier'
'Maman Cochet'
'Souvenir de Mme. Leonie Viennot'
'Mrs. B. R. Cant'
'Niles Cochet'
'Mrs. Dudley Cross'
'Lady Hillingdon'
'Rosette Delizy'
"McClinton Tea"

Early Hybrid Teas
'La France'
'Lady Waterlow'
'Belle Portugaise'
'Radiance'
'Red Radiance'
'Climbing Étoile de Holland'
'Crimson Glory'
'Lafter'

Bourbons
'Souvenir de la Malmaison'
'Kronprinzessin Viktoria'
'Climbing Souvenir de la Malmaison'
'Louise Odier'
'Zéphirine Drouhin'
'Mme. Isaac Pereire'
'Mme. Ernst Calvat'
'Variegata di Bologna'
"Maggie"

Hybrid Perpetuals
'Rose du Roi'
'Rose de Rescht'
'Marquise Bocella'
'Baronne Prevost'
'Géant des Batailles'
'General Jacqueminot'
'Comte de Chambord'
'Reine des Violettes'
'Souvenir du Docteur Jamain'
'Baroness Rothschild'
'Paul Neyron'
'American Beauty'
'Climbing American Beauty'
'Ulrich Brünner Fils'
'Marchioness of Londonderry'
'Frau Karl Druschki'

Polyanthas
'Cécile Brünner'
'Climbing Cécile Brünner'
'Perle d'Or'
'Marie Pavié'
'Clotilde Soupert'
'Climbing Clotilde Soupert'

'Tip Top'
'La Marne'
'Mevrouw Nathalie Nypels'
'The Fairy'
'Jean Mermoz'
'China Doll'
'Climbing Pinkie'
"Caldwell Pink"

Hybrid Musks
'Aglaia'
'Trier'
'Danaë'
'Prosperity'
'Vanity'
'Nur Mahal'
'Penelope'
'Cornelia'
'Bishop Darlington'
'Felicia'
'Autumn Delight'
'Skyrocket'
'Belinda'
'Ballerina'
'Buff Beauty'

'Erfurt'
'Will Scarlet'
'Wind Chimes'
'Lavender Lassie'

Shrub and Climbing Roses from Assorted Classes
'Harison's Yellow'
'May Queen'
'Evangeline'
'Grüss an Aachen'
'Silver Moon'
'Baby Faurax'
'Mary Wallace'
'Mme. Gregoire Staechelin'
'Blaze'
'Betty Prior'
'New Dawn'
'Leverkusen'
'Meg'
'Dortmund'
'Belinda's Rose'
'Gene Boerner'
'Canterbury'
"Petite Pink Scotch"

Suggested Roses for Various Landscape Needs

Roses Useful as Low Hedges (1'–3')
'Baby Faurax'
'Betty Prior'
"Caldwell Pink"
'Cécile Brünner'
'China Doll'
'Cramoisi Supérieur'
'Ducher'
'Grüss an Aachen'
'Hermosa'
"Highway 290 Pink Buttons"
'Jean Mermoz'

'Louis Philippe'
'Marie Pavié'
"Martha Gonzales"
'Perle d'Or'
'Petite Pink Scotch'
'Tip Top'

Roses Useful as Medium Hedges (5'–6')
'Archduke Charles'
'Ballerina'
'Banshee'
'Belinda'

'Belinda's Rose'
'Bishop Darlington'
'Buff Beauty'
'Champneys' Pink Cluster'
'Cherokee'
'Climbing Cécile Brünner'
'Climbing Pinkie'
'Cornelia'
'Cramoisi Supérieur'
'Ducher'
'Danaë'
'Duchesse de Brabant'

'Erfurt'
'Felicia'
'Gene Boerner'
'Hermosa'
'La Marne'
'Lavender Lassie'
'Louis Philippe'
'Mary Washington'
'Mrs. B. R. Cant'
'Mrs. Dudley Cross'
'Mutabilis'
'Nastarana'
"Natchitoches Noisette"
'Nur Mahal'
'Old Blush'
"Old Gay Hill Red China"
"Pam's Pink"
'Penelope'
'Radiance'
'Red Radiance'
'Rosa Mundi'
'Russell's Cottage Rose'
'Skyrocket'
'Swamp Rose'
'Vanity'
'Wind Chimes'

Roses Useful as Large Hedges
'Ballerina'
'Basye's Purple Rose'
'Belinda'
'Canterbury'
'Climbing Cécile Brünner'
'Cornelia'
'Felicia'
'Mermaid'
'Mme. Isaac Pereire'
'Mutabilis'
'Swamp Rose'
'Trier'
'Ulrich Brünner Fils'
'Zéphirine Drouhin'

Roses of Outstanding Vigor
'Cherokee'
'Climbing Cécile Brünner'
'Fortuniana'
'Lady Banks' Rose'—yellow and white
'Lafter'
'Mermaid'
'New Dawn'
'Silver Moon'

Roses Having Attractive Hips
'Ballerina'
'Belinda'
'Danaë'
'Dortmund'
'Felicia'
'Jeanne d'Arc'
'Mme. Gregoire Staechelin'
'Nastarana'
'Old Blush'
'Penelope'
R. setigera
Russell's Cottage Rose
'Sweetbrier'
'Trier'
'Wind Chimes'

Roses of Outstanding Fragrance
'Aglaia'
'Aimée Vibert'
'American Beauty'
'Autumn Damask'
'Baby Faurax'
'Banshee'
'Baroness Rothchild'
'Basye's Purple Rose'
'Belinda's Rose'
'Buff Beauty'
'Céline Forestier'
'Celsiana'
'Champneys' Pink Cluster'
'Climbing Etoile de Holland'
'Clotilde Soupert'
'Comte de Chambord'
'Crimson Glory'

'Devoniensis'
'Duchesse de Brabant'
'Felicia'
'Fortuniana'
'Gloire de Dijon'
'Géant des Batailles'
'Grüss an Aachen'
'Jaune Desprez'
'Jeanne d'Arc'
'Kazanlik'
'La France'
'Lamarque'
'La Reine Victoria'
'Lavender Lassie'
'Louise Odier'
"Maggie"
'Maréchal Niel'
"McClinton Tea"
'Mermaid'
'Mme. Alfred Carrière'
'Mme. Ernst Calvat'
'Mme. Gregoire Staechelin'
'Mme. Isaac Pereire'
'Mme. Louis Leveque'
'Marie Pavié'
'Marquise Bocella'
'Mary Washington'
'Mrs. B. R. Cant'
'Musk Rose'
'Paul Neyron'
'Radiance'
'Red Radiance'
R. multiflora 'Carnea'
'Rose du Roi'
'Rose de Rescht'
'Reine des Violettes'
'Salet'
'Sombreuil'
'Souvenir du Docteur Jamain'
'Souvenir de la Malmaison'
'Swamp Rose'
'Trier'
'Ulrich Brünner Fils'
'Variegata di Bologna'
'William Allen Richardson'
'Zéphirine Drouhin'

Thornless . . . or Nearly Thornless Roses
'Climbing Pinkie'
'Lady Banks' Rose'—white and yellow
'Marie Pavié'
'Mrs. Dudley Cross'
'Paul Neyron'
R. setigera serena
'Swamp Rose'
'Zéphirine Drouhin'

Roses for Pergolas, Pillars, Gazebos, and Posts
'Aglaia'
'Aimée Vibert'
'Anemone Rose'
'Ballerina'
'Baronne Prevost'
'Belinda'
'Belle Portugaise'
'Blaze'
'Céline Forestier'
'Champneys' Pink Cluster'
'Claire Jacquier'
'Climbing American Beauty'
'Climbing Cécile Brünner'
'Climbing Crimson Glory'
'Climbing Etoile de Holland'
'Climbing Souvenir de la Malmaison'
'Cornelia'
'Devoniensis'
'Dortmund'
'Erfurt'
'Evangeline'
'Felicia'
'Fortune's Double Yellow'
'Fortuniana'
'Gloire de Dijon'
'Harison's Yellow'
'Jaune Desprez'
'Jeanne d'Arc'
'Lady Banks' Rose'—white and yellow
'Lavender Lassie'
'Leverkusen'
"Maggie"
'Mary Wallace'
'May Queen'

'Mermaid'
'Mme. Gregoire Staechelin'
'Mme. Alfred Carrière'
'New Dawn'
'Nur Mahal'
'Prosperity'
'Rêve d'Or'
R. anemoneflora
R. eglanteria
R. laevigata
R. moschata
R. multiflora 'Carnea'
R. multiflora 'Platyphylla'
'Silver Moon'
'Sombreuil'
'Souvenir de Mme. Leonie Viennot'
'Trier'
'Variegata di Bologna'
'William Allen Richardson'
'Zéphirine Drouhin'

Dark Rose and Red Roses
'American Beauty'
'Blaze'
'Bon Silène'
'Climbing American Beauty'
'Climbing Etoile de Holland'
'Cramoisi Supérieur'
'Dortmund'
'Géant des Batailles'
'General Jacqueminot'
'General Schablikine'
'Louis Philippe'
"Maggie"
"Martha Gonzales"
'Monsieur Tillier'
'Mrs. B. R. Cant'
Nur Mahal'
"Old Gay Hill Red China"
'Red Radiance'
'Rose de Rescht'
'Rose du Roi'
'Skyrocket'
'Souvenir du Docteur Jamain'
'Ulrich Brünner Fils'
'Will Scarlet'

Pink, Purple, and Lavender Roses
'Anemone Rose'
'Baby Faurax'
'Ballerina'
'Banshee'
'Basye's Purple Rose'
'Baroness Rothschild'
'Belinda'
'Canterbury'
'Catherine Mermet'
'Cécile Brünner'
'Chestnut Rose'
'Climbing Cécile Brünner'
'Climbing Pinkie'
'Clotilde Soupert'
'Comte de Chambord'
'Duchess de Brabant'
'Erfurt'
'Evangeline'
'Felicia'
'Gene Boerner'
'Grüss an Aachen'
"Highway 290 Pink Buttons"
'Jean Mermoz'
'Lady Waterlow'
'La France'
'La Marne'
'Lavender Lassie'
'Marie Pavié'
'Marquise Bocella'
'Mary Wallace'
'May Queen'
'Mevrouw Nathalie Nypels'
'New Dawn'
'Old Blush'
"Pam's Pink"
'Paul Neyron'
'Petite Pink Scotch'
'Souvenir de Mme. Leonie Viennot'
'Swamp Rose'
'Radiance'
'Reine des Violettes'
'Russell's Cottage Rose'
'Souvenir de la Malmaison'
'The Fairy'

'Ulrich Brünner Fils'
'Wind Chines'

Roses Having White or White-Blend Flowers
'Aglaia'
'Aimée Vibert'
'Autumn Delight'
'Ducher'
'Evangeline'
'Fortuniana'
'Jeanne d'Arc'
'Kronprinzessin Viktoria'
'Lady Banks' Rose'—white
'Lamarque'
'Madame Plantier'
'Mme. Joseph Schwartz'
'Nastarana'
'Prosperity'
'Silver Moon'
'Sombreuil'
'Trier'

Roses Having Yellow or Yellow-Blend Flowers
'Aglaia'
'Buff Beauty'
'Céline Forestier'
'Claire Jacquiere'
'Harison's Yellow'
'Isabella Sprunt'
'Jaune Desprez'
'Lady Banks' Rose'—yellow
'Lady Hillingdon'
'Leverkusen'
'Maréchal Niel'
'Marie van Houtte'
'Mermaid'
'Mrs. Dudley Cross'
'Perle des Jardins'
'Rêve d'Or'
'Safrano'

'Jeanne d'Arc' is a pure white rose with an outstanding fragrance.

Mail Order Sources for Old Garden Roses

The following list of mail order nurseries and plant societies is included to assist you in locating plants included in the text that may be unavailable locally. Some of the nurseries offer beautiful and interestingly written catalogs for which there is sometimes a small charge. It is suggested that when corresponding with nurseries or plant societies you enclose a stamped, self-addressed envelope. This list is by no means complete, but is included to assist you in furthering your special gardening interests.

Antique Rose Emporium
Rt. 5, Box 143
Brenham, Texas 77833
(409) 836-9051
Own-root old garden roses and perennials. Color catalog $3.00. Also retail at garden center, Independence, Texas.

Country Heritage Roses
Rt. 2, Box 1401
Scurry, Texas 75158
(214) 452-3380
Own-root. Free list. Southeast of Dallas about 60 miles on Texas FM 148.

Donovan's Roses
P.O. Box 37800
Shreveport, Louisiana 71133
Free list.

Forest Farm
990 Tetherow Rd.
Williams, Oregon 97544
(503) 846-6963
Shrubs and species roses. Catalog $1.50.

Greenmantle Nursery
3010 Ettersburg Rd.
Garberville, California 95440
(707) 986-7504
Old garden roses—budded; shrubs. Catalog $3.00. Price list—SASE.

Hastings—Seedsmen to the South
434 Marietta St. N.W., P.O. Box 4274
Atlanta, Georgia 30302
(404) 524-8861
Modern, shrub, and climbing roses. General nursery. Free catalog.

Heritage Rose Gardens
16831 Mitchell Creek Dr.
Ft. Bragg, California 95437
Own-root, two-year-old field-grown. Old garden roses. Catalog $1.00.

High Country Rosarium
1717 Downing Street
Denver, Colorado 80218
(303) 832-4026
Own-root and tissue culture. Old garden roses. Free catalog.

Historical Roses
1657 West Jackson St.
Painesville, Ohio 44077
Old garden, shrub, and modern roses. Two-year budded, field-grown. Free price list.

Hortico Roses
Robson Rd., RR #1
Watersdown, Ontario, Canada LoR-2Ho
(416) 689-6984
Modern, shrub roses, climbers, and groundcover. Free illustrated catalog. Ships to USA.

Liggett's Rose Nursery
1206 Curtiss Ave.
San Jose, California 95125
One- and two-year-old budded plants. Free price list.

Lowe's Own-Root Roses
6 Sheffield Rd.
Nashua, New Hampshire 03062
Custom growing old garden roses. Price list $1.00.

Pickering Nurseries, Inc.
670 Kingston Rd. (Hwy #21)
Pickering, Ontario, Canada L1V 1A6
(416) 839-2111
Modern, climbing, shrub, and antique roses.
Fall shipping. Color catalog $1.00.

Roses of Yesterday and Today, Inc.
802 Brown's Valley Rd.
Watsonville, California 97076
Old garden roses. Collector's catalog $2.00.

Rose Acres
6641 Crystal Boulevard
Diamond Springs, California 95619
(916) 626-1722
SASE for free list.

Wayside Gardens
1 Garden Lane
Hodges, South Carolina 29695-0001
1-800-845-1124
Modern and some old garden roses, shrubs, perennials, etc.

Yesterday's Rose
572 Las Colindas Road
San Rafael, California 94903.

Overseas Ordering

Not all growers will ship individual orders to the USA, but there are a few who do. Three of the most popular sources are listed. If seriously considering such an order, plan well ahead and be sure to know the necessary requirements. A special USDA permit is needed which may take several months to secure. A special rose bed is required for a quarantine period. Send for catalogs.

David Austin Roses
Bowling Green Lane
Albrighton, Wolverhampton, England WV7 3HB
Minimum order $50.

Peter Beales Roses
London Road, Attleborough
Norfolk, England NR17 1AY
Minimum order $50 and 10% surcharge.

Cants of Colchester Ltd
The Old Rose Gardens
London Road, Stanway, Colchester, Essex, England CO3 5UP
Export orders, prepayment in sterling from new customers requested.

Sources for Information

Heritage Roses Group
Mitzi VanSant, South Central U.S. Editor
810 East 30th Street
Austin, Texas 78705

The Old Texas Rose (quarterly newsletter)
Mrs. Margaret P. Sharpe
9426 Kerrwood
Houston, Texas 77080

The Yellow Rose (monthly newsletter)
Joe M. Woodard
8636 Sans Souci Drive
Dallas, Texas 75238

Bev Dobson's Combined Rose List
(a source for locating any commercially
 propagated rose)
215 Harriman Road,
Irvington, New York 10533

The Heritage Rose Foundation
Charles A. Walker, Jr.
1512 Gorman Street
Raleigh, North Carolina 27606

The American Rose Society
P.O. Box 30,000
Shreveport, Louisiana 71130

The Royal National Rose Society
Chiswell Green, St. Albans
Herts, AL2 3NR
England
Telephone (0727) 50461

Ikebana International
Chapter 12 of Ikebana International
℅ Houston Garden Center
1500 Hermann Drive
Houston, Texas 77004

Sources for Rose Crafts

Roberta Moffitt
P.O. Box 3597
Wilmington, DE 19807
Flower drying supplies, dried flowers and leaves,
flower seeds, craft items, books on rose crafts.

Tom Thumb Workshops
Rt. 13, P.O. Box 357
Mappsville, VA 23407
Dried flowers, cones and pods, craft accessories,
flower presses, wreaths and hearts, dried spices,
potpourri containers, essential oils, fragrance
beads, books, illustrated how-tos, gift items.

Intercontinental Fragrances, Inc.
800 Victoria
Houston, TX 77022
Wholesale only. Minimum order $25.00

Ye Seekers
9336 Westview
Houston, TX 77055
Dried flowers and herbs, fragrant oils, fixatives,
potpourris.

A Moveable Feast
3827 Dunlavy
Houston, TX 77006
Dried herbs, spices, potpourri materials, fixatives.

San Lorenzo of Texas
6111 Skyline Drive
Houston, TX 77057
Floral wire, spray paints, ribbon, wreath forms,
foam sheets and objects, containers, craft
tools and supplies.

Craftex Wholesale Distributor
7215 Ashcroft
Houston, TX 77081
Also sells retail. Craft items, tools, and
supplies of all kinds.

Garden Ridge Pottery & World Imports
1150 Silber Road
Houston, TX 77055 (Warehouse)
Retail stores: Interstate 10 at Fry Road, Houston,
TX; 431 Airtex, Humble, TX. Craft items, baskets,
florist foams, wires, tapes, ribbons, containers
of all types.

Caswell-Massey Catalog Division
111 8th Avenue
New York, NY 10011
Retail stores: Atlanta, GA; Washington, DC;
San Francisco, CA; Boston, MA.
Dried flowers, fixatives, essences.

'Rosa Mundi,' in the pleasure garden at Mount
Vernon, is a major attraction each year in late
April and May.

BIBLIOGRAPHY

Affleck, Thomas. *Southern Rural Almanac*. 1860. Found in the Louisiana and Lower Mississippi Valley Collections. LSU Libraries, Louisiana State University, Baton Rouge, Louisiana.

Beales, Peter. *Classic Roses*. New York: Henry Holt & Co., 1985

Bunyard, Edward A. *Old Garden Roses*. New York: Earl M. Coleman Publishing, 1978.

Christopher, Thomas. *In Search of Lost Roses*. New York: Summit Books, 1989.

Drennan, Georgia Torrey. *Everblooming Roses For the Outdoor Garden of the Amateur, Their Culture, Habits, Description, Care, Nativity, Parentage*. Duffield & Co., New York, 1912.

Fagan, Gwen. *Roses at the Cape of Good Hope*. Capetown: Breestraat-Publikasies, 1988.

Fortune, Robert. "A Letter from Robert Fortune." *Journal of the Royal Horticultural Society*. Vol. 6, 1851.

Gault and Synge. *Dictionary of Roses in Colour*. London: Michael Joseph, 1971.

Griffiths, Trevor. *My World of Old Roses*. London: Whitcouls Publishers, 1983.

Hole, Dean S. Reynolds. *Our Gardens*. 1899.

Jekyll, Gertrude and Edward Mawley. *Roses for English Gardens*. London: Country Life, 1922. Reprint. Woodridge, Suffolk: Baron Publishing Co.

Keays, Ethelyn Emery. *Old Roses*. 1935. Reprint. New York: Earl M. Coleman Publishing, 1978.

Krussman, Gerd. *The Complete Book of Roses*. Portland: Timber Press, 1981.

Prince, William Robert. *Prince's Manual of Roses*. Stanfordville, New York: Earl M. Coleman, Publisher, 1979. (A facsimile of the 1846 original.)

Shephard, Roy. *History of the Rose*. Simpkin, Marshall and Hamilton, Kent & Co., 1903.

Thomas, Graham Stuart. *The Old Shrub Roses*. London: J. M. Dent & Sons, Ltd., 1983.

Thomas, Graham Stuart. *Shrub Roses of Today*. London: J. M. Dent & Sons, Ltd., 1980.

Welch, William. *Perennial Garden Color*. Dallas: Taylor Publishing Company, 1989.

INDEX

Photo Credits

All photographs in *Antique Roses for the South* are by the author except as noted here:

Marion L. Brandes, Jr. 5, 23, 40, 46, 115, 163, 178

S. J. Derby 55, 57, 59, 60, 61, 63, 66, 67, 69, 70, 72, 73, 75, 79, 81, 147

Michelle Caldwell 159

S.J. Derby and Margaret Sharpe 82, 86, 88, 89, 93, 95, 96, 97, 98, 99, 101, 103, 106

Christine M. Douglas 33, 36, 39

D. Greg Grant 5, 26, 27, 33, 43, 108, 116, 135, 139

Jonathan Hillyer 98, 99, 103

Virginia Hopper 173

Ruth Knopf 34, 40, 41, 144, 181, 182, 183

Dr. John Lipe 34

Pamela A. Puryear 15, 16, 130, 147, 154, 159, 160

Stephen Scanniello 42, 168, 179